PUPPY TRAINING: A STEP-BY-STEP PROGRAM

PUPPY TRAINING, PUPPY POTTY TRAINING AND CRATE TRAINING FOR PUPPIES & BONUS PUPPY SLEEP TRAINING PROGRAM

ETHAN ADRIAN

CONTENTS

PUPPY TRAINING

POTTY TRAINING A PUPPY

PUPPY CRATE TRAINING

PUPPY SLEEP TRAINING

A step-by-step program, so your pup will understand you & **BONUS 1-WEEK PLAN**

PUPPY TRAINING

HOW TO HOUSEBREAK YOUR PUPPY IN JUST 7 DAYS

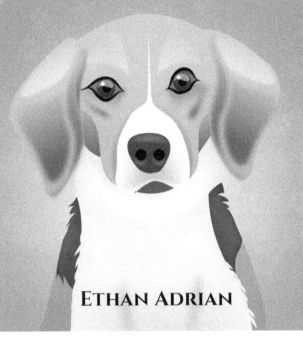

ETHAN ADRIAN

1. BOOK DESCRIPTION

Do you love puppies? Would love to a have a decent pup with good behaviors?

You have landed to the right guide book, all the training guidelines and lessons are properly written to help you ease your puppy training sessions.

Although it might be tedious but bear in mind that there is nothing like a smooth mountain, persistent and patience are all needed.

This book brings together different puppy training methods and techniques which are proven to work best for your pup. It also provides best and successful methods, with easy-to-follow ways to assist a pup in developing clean living habits and a feeling of security in his new environment.

As a puppy owner, **you will learn** helpful tips such as:

- Importance of having a puppy
- What you need before you start
- Health Check
- Understanding How the Puppies mind works
- Different kind of breeds
- First commands, threats, and feeding
- Bedtime routines and much more

2. KNOW AND EXAMINE YOUR PUPPY

2.1. What you need before you start

Training a puppy is hard work; you should always do your research before getting a puppy. Make sure everyone in the house is aware of what the puppy is and is not allowed to do.

Finding a local professional trainer with good reviews is a good place to start if this is your first puppy. Having a professional there will help you best cope with your little fur ball and learn the steps to having a well behaved, calm dog who's always under control.

2.2. HEALTH CHECK

You know how you couldn't sleep when you're not feeling well? It's the same for puppies, too.

The first thing that you have to keep in mind is that **a puppy's health should be in tip-top shape** because if not, you really would not be able to feed him well and help him to sleep. The pointers below will help you understand whether or not your puppy's health is in check:

- **Eyes** - Let's start with the eyes. Remember that a healthy puppy has eyes that are shiny and clear, without any discharge, or the slightest form of cloudiness.
- **Ears** - Another easy way of seeing whether or not a puppy is healthy is by checking his ears. A puppy's ears have to look and smell clean, and there should not be any redness or inflammation outside or inside the ears. You'll know that a puppy is suffering from an infection if his ears are malodorous and if you see some yellow or brown discharge.

- **Nose** - When a puppy's nose is slightly moist, it means that he is healthy, and sweating in a good way. However, you should take note that his nose does not have to be wet, and there has to be no form of discharge there. N.B.: Persistent sniffing and sneezing are big signs that a puppy is not in good shape.

- **Coat and Skin** – In addition, you have to check if the puppy's coat is actually soft, and it also has to be shiny. Check if there are any flakes around. This is a sign that he might be infected with something, or that his coat has been irritated by harsh sunlight.

- **Other things** you could check regarding skin are sores, bumps, redness, patches, and missing hair. The coat and skin also should not smell pungent. Fleas and ticks may also be around, so always make sure to check for them.

- **Abdomen** - It is okay to feel the puppy's ribs, but make sure that the ribs do not poke out. Otherwise, it is a sign that the puppy is malnourished. A round tummy is also good, but it should never be swollen, and your dog also should not be potbellied.

- **Rear End** - Of course, you also have to check your puppy's butt. Make sure it is clean, and that it's free from any fecal matter or debris of any sort.

- **Behavior** - And finally, a puppy's behavior also comes into play. It is normal for a puppy to be sleepy, but never lethargic. Puppies are naturally playful, and friendly to their littermates. In case they begin to isolate themselves, it means they may not be feeling well, and that they're lonely. And, a healthy puppy is one who's excited to eat, not one who does not even mind food on his bowl.

2.3. FIRST VETERINARY EXAM

It's also important that you **bring your puppy to the vet** for his first general veterinary exam. This is done to help determine the health condition of your lovely pet, and if he's experiencing any illnesses and the like. While there, you can expect the vet to:

- **Check your puppy's ears** to see if they look and smell right and that he's not suffering from infections of any kind.
- **Check the puppy's temperature**, which normally ranges from 100 to 125 F. Breathing and pulse rate will be checked, too.
- **Check your puppy's weight**. He'll know if your puppy is normal, underweight, or overweight.
- **Listen for any abnormalities** in the heart and lungs, as well as feel organs, and check for palpitations.
- **Check the puppy's mouth** and see if teeth and gums are in normal condition.
- **Check eyes**, skin, nose, and anal region to see if there are signs of parasites or diseases.
- **Check the puppy's genitals**. For females, he'll check for

signs of infection or discharge. For males, he'll check if both testicles are present.

If you see that your puppy is experiencing things that you are meant to be aware of, take that as a sign that it's time to bring him to the vet. Signs that your puppy needs immediate care are listed below:

- Any form of eye injury. Nothing is considered "mild" when it comes to that.
- Hives, swelling, and any other allergic reactions, especially those in the belly.
- Signs of pain, such as loss of appetite, restlessness, lethargy, increased body temperature, labored breathing and panting.
- Respiratory problems, such as trouble breathing, or chronic coughing.
- Animal bites, wounds, lacerations, especially those that are open.
- Suspected poisoning, such as indigestion of human medication, snail or rodent bait, and antifreeze.
- Diarrhea or vomiting, especially if he experiences it more than twice or thrice in an hour.
- Any form of collapse, fainting, or seizure.

Remember that prevention is always better than cure, and this way, you'll be able to focus on improving his sleeping habits, and his health, in general!

Keep all household cleaners and chemicals put away in an area your puppy can't get to, including your garage. There are many plants that are toxic to dogs. The parts that are toxic on the plant can be the leaves, roots, or bulbs. If your puppy is sick and you, or your vet, can't figure out why? Suggest the possibility of ingestion of a toxic plant. Be careful using herbicides, pesticides, and insecticides. Your puppy could lick a leaf or chew on a stick that was sprayed with one of these and become seriously ill.

Be sure to get copies of your puppy's health record when you pick him up from the breeder, shelter, or whoever you get him from. Most vets will want to see it because it may contain some information someday that may save your puppy's life. If you own a large breed puppy, wait until your vet gives the "okay" before you begin jogging with him and don't allow him to slip on slippery floors. This helps with proper hip development.

For vaccinations, give each shot at two-week intervals. For example, if you give your puppy his DHPP, wait two weeks to give him another shot. The same goes for worming medications. This will help lower the stress to your puppy's system and to know which shot or medication caused your puppy to have a reaction.

If you buy a purebred puppy, be sure his dew claws have been removed. These are the claws that are on the inside of the leg, back or front. It can be very painful for a puppy to catch his dew claw on something and have it ripped out.

Get to know your puppy and his habits. It will be easier to notice if he's sick or injured in any way. Give your puppy vaccinations yourself. Many pet supply catalogs offer vaccines and tell you exactly what to give and where to give it. Talk to your vet about which brands he recommends and questions you may have. Giving vaccinations yourself can save you a considerable amount of money. The more to spend on puppy toys!

If a puppy is ill or injured, he may bite. Keep this in mind if your puppy bites for no apparent reason. If your puppy eats feces, be sure your feeding quality food and he doesn't have worms. If those checkouts, just keep your yard clean. He can't eat what's not there! If you have a hard time giving your puppy pills, try storing them in or near his puppy food. The pills will probably absorb the smell of the puppy food making them easier to give your puppy.

Does your puppy scoot around the floor in a sitting position? He probably needs to have his anal sacs emptied. Do this yourself by gently, but firmly, squeezing on either side of the anus. Have plenty of paper towels handy. It's a dirty job, so it is highly recommended having your vet do it. If your puppy looks or acts seriously ill or injured, call your vet.

Never allow your puppy to stick his head out the window when you're driving down the road. All sorts of debris can get into his eyes. It's safest to leave the window down a few inches and let him feel the air against his face from inside the car.

Never leave your puppy inside a vehicle when it's hot out. It only takes a few minutes for your puppy to die from the heat. Leave your puppy home where he will be cool and comfortable, and alive.

Seriously consider spaying or neutering your puppy within his first year. There are many advantages to this, including behavioral and medical. In females, mammary cancer, which is one of the top cancers in females not spayed, is nearly eliminated.

Uterine cancer, uterine infections, and ovarian cancer are also nearly eliminated in spayed females. Spayed females also have no desire to mate; therefore they won't be tempted to wander in search of a mate. By neutering your male puppy, you eliminate the risk of prostate problems, rectal tumors, and testicular cancer. He will also be less likely to roam since he'll have no desire to mate. Neutering can also make him less aggressive toward other male dogs. And the biggest point of spaying and neutering is that you won't have any unexpected or unwanted puppies.

Here are some different ways to exercise your puppy: walking on lead, free running in an open field, playing fetch, running up and down the stairs, and playing with a plastic ball that can be batted around, but not picked up or gripped in the mouth.

3. KNOW YOUR BREED

3.1. Understanding how the puppy's mind works

It is important for you to bond with your puppy and know what it wants from you or to do. Massaging and grooming your puppy is an excellent way to bond with him. Start with his head then go to his ears, neck, shoulders, front legs, back, sides, and hips. You'll notice him starting to nod off and close his eyes when you start. I've actually seen a few puppies fall over they were so relaxed!

When your puppy bows down (front legs parallel to the ground, hind legs perpendicular to the ground), he's telling you he wants to play. Give him a command, and when he does it, play with him. Keep your puppy under control at all times for his safety and others'. This means keeping him on a leash when outside.

Never take your puppy for a walk down the street without him being leashed. Someday, something may scare him or invite him to chase and he may get hit by a car. Sure you may want to show off how well your puppy heels or how intelligent your puppy is, but the consequences aren't worth it.

Leave the door to your puppy's crate open when he's not in it. Most puppies will view the crate as their den and go in there on their own when they're tired or just need a break from everything.

3.2. WHAT TO KNOW ABOUT BREEDS

Purebred - A purebred puppy is one whose parents are both of the same recognized breeds — for example, both parents are Collies or both parents are Dalmatians.

Registered - A registered puppy is one that's purebred and has a record of his birth and his parents' births kept by an organization specializing in registering dogs. For example, both parents are registered German Shepherds and the litter has been registered with the appropriate kennel club or breed club, the puppies are considered registered.

Pedigreed - A pedigree is a record of a puppy's ancestors, usually written as a family tree. Some breeders furnish a pedigree of their own. A certified pedigree can also be ordered from the kennel or breed club with which the puppy is registered. A pedigreed puppy is one for which such an ancestry record has been kept.

Mixed Breed - A mixed-breed puppy is one whose parents are from more than one recognized breed or from undetermined parentage. For example, his father might be a Labrador Retriever and his mother an Irish Setter, or one or both of his parents themselves might be mixed breeds. Many times no one has any idea what a dog's ancestors were because as far back as anyone can remember, they were mixed breeds. Mixed-breed dogs are sometimes called mongrels or mutts.

Crossbred - A crossbred puppy is one whose parents are of two or more different breeds, but their mating was planned deliberately by professional breeders to produce a new breed.

Inbred or Line bred - Inbred or line bred puppies are those whose parents are of the same breed and closely related by family kinship. Experienced dog breeders mate such dogs to reinforce particular inherited traits.

3.3. Considerations between mixed breeds and pure breeds

For a willing puppy owner, it is important to consider the following facts on mixed breeds and purebred puppies.

Mixed Breeds

A mixed-breed puppy or his parents are not of the same breed. You may not be able to find out what breed or mixture of breeds his parents are. If he's a puppy, you may have to guess what he will look like as an adult, how large he will get, and what characteristics he may have inherited from his parents. A cute, cuddly little puppy of eight weeks might turn out to weigh 10 pounds or 100 pounds.

Mixed breeds generally seem to have fewer of the inherited health complications that are common in certain pure breeds. These health complications include deafness, early cancer, and hip dysplasia. Mixed breeds probably have fewer inherited health complications because both parents are not the same breed and are less apt to carry the matching problem genes.

How Big Will that Mixed-Breed Puppy Get?

One way to get an idea of whether a puppy will grow up into a large or small dog is to look at his bone structure, especially in his legs and paws. A puppy with a large bone structure and heavy legs and paws will most likely grow up to be much larger and heavier than one of the same age with fine bones and small legs and paws. Some breeds that have a fine bone structure, however, grow up to be very tall; the Greyhound is an example.

Pure Breeds

Purebred dogs were bred by people to have specific characteristics of the structure, hair coat, color, size, abilities, and temperament.

The genetic makeup of the pure breed is easily changed by selective breeding. By choosing particular physical and character traits, and then breeding dogs that have those traits, people have developed purebred dogs that can perform amazing roles.

Dogs have been specially bred to hunt game, track prisoners, guard and defend property and people, herd cattle and sheep, work with police, run races, sniff for drugs and other illegal items, dig out badgers, seek out rats, provide companionship, and more.

3.4. WHEN TO BEGIN TRAINING?

Puppy training is an activity that has an immense contribution to a dog's life in terms of behavior and response.

Puppy training is a very important aspect in the growth and development of a dog. This is due to the fact that it plays a great role in determining the manner in which the puppy will behave once it is a fully grown dog. It is, therefore, important to introduce your puppy to such training at a very young age, probably at the tenth week.

4. GETTING STARTED

4.1. First day at home

Be sure to puppy proof your home before you bring your puppy home.

The easiest way to do this is to lie on the floor in each room and scan the area from the floor to about 2-3 feet up.

Hide electric cords, put up plants and breakables, put away any rodent poisons or traps and cleaners, and anything else within your puppy's reach that you don't want to be eaten, destroyed, or harm your puppy.

4.2. FIRST COMMANDS, THREATS, AND FEEDING

Be consistent when training your puppy or he will get confused as to when or if to listen.

If you tell him to sit, make him sit.

If you tell him to stay, make him stay.

If you don't want him on the couch, never let him on the couch.

If you don't want him jumping on you, don't let him jump up.

You have to do it when it needs to be done, or you'll pay the price tenfold! Basic commands are the foundation of obedience training.

You could sign your puppy up for professional obedience training lessons, but you may want to attempt teaching the commands on your own first. If your puppy catches on quickly, then you could save some money by at least teaching the basic skills on your own.

Following are effective strategies for teaching all of the basic commands. **Remember to use the same word** every time you work on a command. Your dog will learn what you want them to do according to that exact sound, so the terms cannot be switched up. Stay consistent!

"Come"

This is typically the first command you will teach your puppy. You can teach it simultaneously with "**sit**" and "**stay.**" You are essentially telling your puppy to come to you. The key is to teach your puppy that coming to you is a pleasant experience. You never call your puppy to you and then put them on a leash, throw them right into the crate, or otherwise send a signal of punishment.

Rather, call them to you and give them a small treat for a prompt response. Love on them. Slip them a small treat. Start by giving treats just for coming when called, and then start giving them only when they come and sit as commanded. Finally, wean out the treats, so they get used to coming just for a pat on the head and a bit of attention.

Work with this command throughout your puppy's life. By adulthood, they should be well trained to come to you on command.

"Sit"

You can use small treats as well as praise and love to get your puppy to come to you and sit on command. Your goal should be to train them to sit and stay, so work with these two commands together. Start by gently pushing down on the backside of the puppy while giving this command. You should only have to do this a couple times before they catch on to what "**sit**" means.

After that, command them to sit after getting their attention and give them a small treat. Start by rewarding just the sit. You can then start rewarding only when they sit and stay for a couple seconds. Start this training at home without any distractions. With time you can practice around other people, in public places, and with other distractions that will make the puppy want to get up and run.

Eventually, you want your puppy to come to you, sit down, and stay put. A well-trained puppy will eventually grow into a well-trained adult dog able to stay by its owner's side even when there are serious distractions, such as a bird playing in a puddle nearby. That level of training takes time, so be patient.

"Shake"

This is probably the easiest trick to teach your puppy. Have your puppy sit in front of you. Tell him "shake" and grab his front paw and give it a gentle shake. Then give him a treat. Do this a couple times. After the fifth or sixth time, tell him "shake" and just put your hand in front of him and see if he'll offer his paw. If he does, really praise him and give him a treat. If not, grab his paw and keep repeating until he'll offer his paw on his own.

4.3. POTTY TRAINING

It is time to potty train your puppy by use Clicker training. This method is based on the popular "**clicker training**". Instead of using the clicker for every aspect of training, you'll be using it for potty training only, thereby increasing its effectiveness. If you don't have a clicker, visit your nearest pet store.

You can use this method whether you have a puppy or dog, work all day or are at home, or if you've already started a different potty training method and it hasn't worked. Simply **throw out the other ideas you've had** about potty training and start fresh. This method is so easy to teach and most puppies and dogs will catch on extremely quickly.

Keep in mind though that your puppy will need to have **a good diet and a strict schedule**. No puppy will become potty trained if he is fed "less than quality" food and if he's fed whenever. You need to be completely dedicated, no matter how tired you are! Remember, a puppy learns only what he has been taught. Your puppy's good behavior, or lack of, reflects directly on you!

Before you begin with this method, you need to set your puppy up for success. Since your puppy is young, chances are he simply can't hold it for more than a few hours at a time. It would be very cruel of us to expect him to hold it all day so be prepared to clean up messes until he's around 3-5 months of age. To help control where he messes in the house you will need to set up a room or a large crate. These will be large enough for him to have areas to play, sleep, and mess. If we don't give him room to do these things he will probably develop the nasty habit of messing where he sleeps. This is a very difficult habit to break so let's prevent it from the very beginning. If you use a room or exercise pen, it will work well if you use a crate for him to sleep in. This will prepare him for when he's older and you want to crate him when you leave.

When you set up the area he will use when alone, be sure he has something comfortable to sleep on, and the material you want him to normally mess on outside. If you want him to always go on the grass, place a piece of sod in his area. One piece should last nearly a week if you just clean up the poop. You want to leave the urine smell in the sod since this will attract your puppy back to the sod. If you prefer he always go on the cement outside, get a thin slab of cement for his area. Again, just clean off the poop and every few days rinse the slab with plain water.

Now we're ready to begin! If you haven't brought your puppy home yet plan on starting this from the second, you pick him up. If you already have your puppy, start this when you'll have a few full days to work on it. First, we need to associate the clicker with some-thing very good. This is one of the few times you'll hear me say to use treats when training, but there is no better reward for a puppy than a tasty treat!

And what behavior other than going to the bathroom outside deserves something this good? Grab your puppy, the clicker, and a few treats you know your puppy likes. It will be advisable to do this outside on the surface you want him to use, at his designated potty spot, since you'll always be clicking and treating his behavior outside.

All you need to do now is click a few times then give him a treat. Choose how many times you'll click the clicker, so he knows what he's doing well every time. Once or twice should suffice. Be sure to only give him a small piece of the treat. Don't give him a whole mouthful.

Continue to click and treat every few minutes. Once he hears the clicks and looks to you for a treat you know, he's caught on. Now we wait until he goes to the bathroom. As soon as he starts to pee or poop click the clicker, however, many times you've decided on. When he's finished, give him a treat and really praise him. Put your clicker away until the next time you take him out to the bathroom. Repeat this every time he goes.

Now you're probably wondering how to handle it when he goes in the house. Well, you do nothing but clean it up.

Provided you click and treat every time he goes to the bathroom outside he will catch on that good things happen when he goes outside, but nothing happens when he goes in the house. Before long, he'll want to go outside all the time to go to the bathroom and get a treat.

By using a few days to get him used to his spot outside on the surface you've chosen, chances are he'll go on that same surface in the house. If he doesn't, try making his indoor mess area a little bigger or placing a small chunk of sod where he's previously gone pee on top of his indoor sod. Before long, you should have a puppy that willingly holds it until he can get outside.

NOTE: Don't expect too much from a puppy under 12-16 weeks old or a small breed puppy, though. Young and very small puppies just aren't physically capable of holding it that long.

This should only be started after at least two weeks of no accidents in the house and your pup letting you know consistently that he needs to go out. We can now assume that your puppy understands that he is expected to go to the bathroom outside and that he'll let you know it, so it should be safe to begin! Start this on a weekend morning or anytime you'll have a few days to dedicate to this.

Take him out as you normally would in the morning. Click and treat as normal for this time. The next time you take him out, don't click but give a treat. Couple this with plenty of praise. Take him back in and wait until the next time he needs to go out. Click and treat for this one. Do the click and treat for every other bathroom break for the rest of the day. If he seems okay with everything and is still going to the door to be let out, with no accidents in the house, we can move on to the next day. If he backslides even one time with either not letting you know he needs to go out or going to the bathroom in the house, go back to click and treating every time. He obviously isn't ready.

Give him a few more days and try again. If everything went smoothly your first day, click and treat every third bathroom break. Continue this for a few days and if all is well, try eliminating the click and treat altogether for one day. If he has accidents in the house go back a step. If all goes well, forget the click and treat for a few days and monitor his behavior. If he seems okay with the new arrangement, pat yourself on the back! You now have a potty trained puppy!

If your puppy makes a mistake in the house, go back one step and continue working on that particular step for a few days. Some puppies may catch on to this right away and others may take weeks or even months. Keep in mind that you shouldn't use the clicker for any other training. You don't want to confuse him, do you?

You can alter this method to fit your needs for other potty training. If you want to train your pup to mess in a litter box, simply click every time he goes in it. Follow the same guidelines, with the exception of teaching him how to let you know he needs to go out. Or if you have a doggy door, you can teach this method with much quicker results. Set your pup's pen up in front of the doggy door when you're gone and he'll be potty trained in no time! First, you must teach him to go out the doggy door. This is a matter of simply coaxing him through it, while you hold it open, to get his dinner. Do this a few times until he seems okay with it. Then close the door and have someone coax him through to the other side. This shouldn't take much more than a few times. When teaching with the use of a doggy door keep in mind that you'll still need to go out with him to click and treat. Let him go out the doggy door and once he's through you simply go out behind out.

Consult your vet if you feel your puppy is going way too much or not enough because some potty training problems are caused by the puppy or dog being sick. Don't expect too much from your puppy either. He's a puppy and will do what comes naturally or what was unintentionally taught to him. It's your job to teach him what is and isn't acceptable behavior. Don't slack off because you feel your puppy is stupid and incapable of learning or because you've just had it with trying to teach him to go outside for three weeks and he's still messing in the house.

All puppies can and will learn if given the proper instruction and time to learn. So get ready to begin properly potty training your puppy! Before we begin, take note of these potty training do's and don'ts.

4.4. POTTY TRAINING DO'S

- Take your puppy out when he wakes up, after eating and drinking, when you first get home, and after play sessions.
- Take him outside through the same door.
- Take him to the same spot.
- Bring him back in through the same door.
- Take your puppy out on a leash.
- Clean up messes inside with a solution of half vinegar and half water.
- Choose a phrase as his "bathroom" signal and use it as soon as you get him to his spot.
- Leave a few stools at his bathroom area.
- Rush your puppy outside if he starts to mess in the house.
- Keep him on a set schedule for feeding, walking, etc.

4.5. Potty Training Don'ts

- Don't rub your puppy's nose in his mess.
- Don't leave him in his crate for longer periods than he can handle.
- Don't scold him for making a mess in the house.

- Don't hit your puppy for messing in the house.
- Don't play with him before he goes to the bathroom.
- Don't let him have the run of the house before he's fully trustworthy.
- Don't scold your puppy if he starts to mess in the house.
- Don't use newspaper when potty training. They're messy and confuse your pup.
- Don't use different doors to take him outside and back in.
- Don't ignore your puppy's need to go out no matter how tired you are.

4.6. THE PUPPY DOORBELL

Once your puppy has had no accidents in the house for at least 2 weeks, **it's time to start teaching** him to let you know when he needs to go out. After teaching him how to let you know he needs to go out, it's time to start eliminating the clicker and treats.

Everyone wants their puppy to notify them when he needs to go out. You'll have to decide how you want your puppy to let you know. Most people don't want their puppies jumping on the door or scratching at the door since this only create damaged doors. The best method to avoid such damages is to **use the puppy door bell**. You simply hang a bell from your door knob; mount it on the wall at your puppy's level. Or you can use another method of teaching your puppy to bark when he needs to go out. However, this method can be difficult to teach since many puppies won't bark until they're older, and some breeds just aren't inclined to bark.

Before you install the doorbell, your puppy needs to know that messing is supposedly done outside only. Your puppy should be fully trustworthy when you're home with him in the house. It works best at this time because your puppy knows he should go outside, but he just doesn't know how to get out. And at this time, he should be old enough to hold it for longer periods, allowing you to take him out at certain times without having to clean up any messes in the house.

Once you've got your bell in place, you'll need to **show your puppy the bell**. Encourage him to sniff it or lick it. If he happens to make it sound off open the door and take him out. If he doesn't make it sound off, you can do it, then open the door and take him out. It also advisable to have your puppy leashed when you practice with the bell, so you have control of him when you take him out. Of course, every time he does something good be sure to praise him; whether he touches the bell, makes it sound off, looks at the door after making noise, anything. Be most lavish with your praise if he rings the bell then looks to the door.

Have him ring the bell every time before you go out and very soon he should catch on that ringing the bell opens the door which allows him to go to the bathroom. Be very vigilant about this and before too long you will hear the bell when you're watching television. This is the time when you really praise and let him know how he is. **Immediately take him outside** to his spot.

4.7. CRATE OR PEN TRAINING

Crate training is one of the most popular forms of puppy training. You purchase a crate of suitable size for your puppy from a pet store and use it to limit the puppy's access to your home. You never want to turn an untrained puppy loose in your home, even for short periods of time.

The puppy does not yet know how to behave in your home and will undoubtedly chew a hole in your couch cushion, tear down the curtains, or scratch a hole in your carpet trying to dig out from under a door.

Crate training confines the puppy when they cannot be directly supervised. If you will be out of the home most of the day to work, it is a good idea to get the puppy used to the crate right away. Just make sure they are never left in the cage so long that they have to potty in the crate.

You can use the crate to help the puppy learn to hold their bladder during potty training, but they should never be left more than four or five hours at a stretch when you first start this training.

The basic premise of **crate training is simple**. When you need to keep the puppy safe from danger and out of trouble, you put them in the crate. You bring them out for feedings and potty breaks, and of course, to play with them and love them. Then they go back into the crate. This continues until they are completely potty trained and can be trusted in your home without direct supervision.

The Secret to Crate Training

Your puppy must see their crate as their **safe place**; **their bed**; **their comfy place** to retire. If they are left in the crate for long periods of time and/or neglected of your love and attention, they will see their crate as a place of punishment. They will fight you every time you try to put them in that crate. They will whine, cry and howl every time they are locked in there.

Crate training will be an option for many of the training strategies presented throughout this book. When considering this option, always keep in mind this secret to crate training. Your training will not be effective if your pup decides the crate is punishment, rather than their safe haven.

When used correctly, **your puppy will love going in his crate** even after he has been turned free to roam the home. They will go to this bed when they are tired, when they want to hide from unusual activity, or just when they want to hide a bone.

4.8. STOP FROM NIPPING OR BITING

Many puppies go through a stage of biting everything from your hand to your stocking feet. As soon as biting begins it should be nipped in the bud, so to speak.

Your puppy doesn't really intend to hurt you when they bite; they explore much of the world with their mouths. When your puppy mouths you pay close attention. When the bite gets too hard or starts to hurt be sure to let out a loud sound. Yelps and "**Ouch**" do well. The startle of volume will make him stop biting. When he releases walk away for a short period of time say 10-20 seconds then resume playing. It takes time, but your puppy will catch on and learn that biting is something he shouldn't do.

Natural Consequences

Allowing your puppy to experience the natural consequences of their feisty behavior is perhaps the most efficient way to teach them to tame this behavior. Naturally, puppies learn not to bite by playing with their parents and litter mates. When they get too rough and hurt each other, they will naturally put one another in place. They learn as they grow **to treat one another with respect** and to play in a gentle, safe manner.

If you have puppies around the same age, then you can simply allow them to play together to start the process of eliminating biting during play. If you have only one puppy, then finding other dogs for them to play with is vital. Just make sure those other dogs are not overly aggressive, as that will teach your puppy to be rougher, rather than gentler.

The Right Response

You have to make sure everyone with access to your puppy responds to a bite or nip in the same manner. You do not want to yell at them, strike them, or throw them into their crate. Even if they bite kind of hard and it hurts, you have to respond with a firm, "**No.**" You can also put them down if they are on your lap, or get up if you are on the floor. Removing yourself from contact with the puppy shows them that the biting and nipping is not acceptable. Importantly, you have to go back and show a bit of love to your puppy, so they know you are not mad at them. It is the behavior you are trying to correct, so your puppy must know you still love them.

Consistency Is Key

You have to respond immediately and in the same manner, every time you see an unacceptable behavior in your puppy. A playful puppy will learn rather quickly that biting a playmate instantly ends the play session. If you can give them active play time with other dogs or puppies as well, they will learn even faster.

4.9. PLAY NICE WITH OTHER DOGS

There are a variety of social problems that can develop if a puppy is not properly socialized early in life. **Some puppies may become fearful** of other dogs, which leads to dog aggression. Other dogs may become overly excited when they do come in contact with other dogs. Many dogs will not know how to properly play with other dogs, so they may struggle to make friends or may anger other dogs as they get older.

The best thing you can do is start exposing your puppy to other dogs of all ages and sizes, as well as humans. Do this as soon as your puppy has received all of their shots and is protected from illnesses other dogs may pass on to them. It is often advised that a puppy is well socialized before they turn five or six months old, so it is never too early to start.

Allow your puppy to interact with other dogs in your home. Just make sure it is supervised and the new puppy is not being treated aggressively, as that passes on aggressive behavior.

Allow them to interact with dogs owned by your friends and relatives. Take them to the dog park. Do not turn them off of the leash until you are confident they can interact with other dogs properly. Try to **keep them with dogs their own size** and age at first. Take them out for walks in a variety of locations. Get them used to seeing other dogs and being in crowds without becoming scared or overly excited.

It is also important to other dogs to walk through your backyard while your puppy is young. This helps them accept the fact that this territory of theirs may occasionally be used by other dogs and that it is okay.

5. BEDTIME ROUTINES

As a puppy owner, it is important to ensure that the puppy has a good and adequate sleep. Just like humans, you could not expect puppies to just go to sleep even if their surroundings are not in a proper condition. The first thing you have to keep in mind is that it is **important to provide them with a clean environment**. This can be achieved by following the following steps:

Provide Them with a Space All Their Own

Puppies need to feel safe and secure in their environment. That is why you have to give them a space in the house that they could consider their own den. It could either be their own room or maybe even place their bed in your bedroom, so they would know that you are around and they are safe.

Keep boundaries from other pets

Sometimes, puppies do not mix well with the other pets you have at home, especially if they're of the other kinds, such as cats. You have to keep in mind that you cannot expect them to just mingle with one another right away. They have to be familiarized with each other's scents first. It is a way of helping them get to know each other.

The sense of ownership is important for pets, too If you get a new puppy and let him stay in the bed that's owned by other pets, your other pets may harbor ill feelings towards you and that is not something you want to happen. Try not to make the pets fight on the get-go. Fighting makes them stressed and does not make it easy for them to sleep.

The Right Bed

Puppies also like sleeping on comfortable beds. Sometimes, the kind of bed they sleep in would determine whether they'd sleep well or not.

5.1. DIFFERENT BEDS SUITABLE FOR PUPPIES

- **Bolster Beds** - Bolster beds are quite comfortable and most puppies feel at home in one. Bolster beds are like padded beds but provide additional support for the puppies because they could rest their heads at elevated angles.
- **Cedar-Filled Beds** - are also padded beds and could be purchased from most pet stores. The difference between these beds and typical padded beds is the fact that cedar-filled beds are created to mask a pet's odor, especially in confined spaces. However, since the bed is trying to mask your pet's odor, the bed emits the smell of cedar and the bed might be a problem if you are not comfortable with that smell. Dogs may also find the smell a bit annoying, and you'd see them roll around a little too much.
- **Cots** - Cots are lifted slightly above the ground and could be placed outside, so that the puppy could have a place to rest outdoors, too. Cots are also recommended for dogs with thick coats because they provide proper air circulation so the dog would not be in heat.
- **Simple Padded** - are the most common kind of pet beds. They're basically just pillows covered with soft and

comfortable materials and are also stuffed, mostly with cotton. They're also the most affordable pet beds, making them a favorite of many pet owners.

- **Orthopedic Beds** - Orthopedic beds are mainly used for old, arthritic dogs. But, if your puppy is suffering from hip dysplasia, or has recently survived an accident, orthopedic beds may help them sleep, too. Orthopedic beds are designed in such a way that the dog's body would not touch the ground so his back would not hurt. They also decrease the amount of cold that a dog feels because of extra padding. This way, his condition would not worsen, and his joints would start recuperating.
- **Corner Bed** - Corner beds are perfect for puppies, and small dog breeds, as well as for houses that are not very spacious because they're meant to fit in the corner of a room.
- **Cave Bed** - Cave beds give some puppies a sense of security because they know they could hide in them. The beds are characterized by having a hood, which makes for easy snuggling.
- **Heated and Cooled Beds** - are special kinds of beds that are meant for puppies who are experiencing medical problems. They could either be cooled or heated, depending on the weather so that the puppy could easily adjust and sleep.
- **Crates** - Crates give the puppy a den-like experience and preferred by most puppy owners. Crates are very crucial in training the puppy how to keep the house in order and not wandering all over the house.

5.2. PLAYPENS

While training your puppy, you can also make use of playpens just to acclimatize your puppy to his new space. Playpens are essential for:

- Helping the puppy separate his thoughts from playtime and sleeping.

- Helping the puppy get to know other pets, without the risk of having them fight because they're in one small area alone.

- Keeping the puppy safe, especially if you're trying to fix some things in the house.

- Helping him enjoy the outdoors, without being at risk of being attacked, or meeting accidents.

5.3. FEEDING TIME

A puppy will also sleep better if you feed him at the right time. This is around 3 to 5 hours before he sleeps.

You can **feed him 2 to 3 hours before he sleeps** but make sure it's nothing too heavy. This is because the puppy's bladder becomes full, and of course, that is a sign that they'll probably wake up to pee or defecate in the middle of the night, which can be inconvenient.

5.4. BRING HIS SECURITY ITEMS WITH YOU

With time, you'll realize that your puppy has certain items that make him feel secure. Usually, it's in the form of a blanket. If you're traveling or going somewhere for the night, and you're bringing your puppy with you, make sure **to bring his security items**, too. This will make it easy for him to sleep. It could also be done when you're bringing him to the vet, and if he has to stay there overnight.

5.5. SIMPLE RULES

In helping your puppy sleep, there are certain things that you have to do. Follow the steps below and you'll surely be able to help your puppy go to bed at the right time and help you catch up on sleep, too!

Fix his bed.

The first thing you have to do is make sure your puppy's bed is made-up. This way, once you bring him inside the room, he'll know that it'll be okay for him to go to sleep and that the day is over.

Go potty!

As mentioned in an earlier chapter, it's always good to bring your puppy to his potty area shortly before going to bed. This way, he would be able to associate this action to the fact that he should do his dirty now, so both of you could go to bed later.

Establish a routine.

You know how you have some kind of routine before going to bed? You can do that for your puppy, too. For example, every night before going to bed, go and give your dog a lukewarm bath or just wash his body with lukewarm cloth. Then, play with him a bit just until he gets tired and then go and give him his blanket or his favorite pillow. This has a lot to do with observation, you see. You'd often notice your being comfortable once his close to a certain toy or certain part of his bed at bed- time. Give him that. Or, you might see him kneading or hugging his bed, or his toys at this time - allow him. This way, he'd know he's safe, and there would be some sense of security. This would then make it easier for him to sleep. When puppies need sleep, they sleep. You may be playing with your puppy one second and the next he's sound asleep. This is what puppies do!

6. COMMON BEHAVIOR ISSUES

6.1. Incessant, whining and howling

There are few things more exhausting than a puppy insistent on howling, whining and barking through the night. You can expect some agitation when you first start crate training a puppy, but **you have to work** with the whining and barking immediately, so you do not reinforce that behavior.

For instance, if you let the puppy out of the crate just to shut them up, you can guarantee they will whine and bark even louder next time. You have reinforced that behavior **by sending the message** that whining and barking brings an exit from the crate.

You first have to ensure that all of the puppy's needs are being met, that they are comfortable in their crate, and that they are not suffering in any manner medically.

You have likely already had the puppy checked out by a vet, so health conditions or internal pain should be ruled out already. Check off the following items just to make sure there is nothing you can do to easily calm your new pup down: **The puppy is being fed adequate**

amounts of food each day. The puppy has been let out to potty within the past few hours.

The crate is large enough for the puppy to stand up and turn around comfortably. There are blankets or bedding in the crate to keep the puppy comfortable and warm.

The puppy is not infested with fleas or ticks and has no rashes or skin irritations. The puppy has been exercised and given ample opportunity to burn off energy before bedtime. You have given the puppy something to chew on if they are teething.

If all of these things have been taken care of and your puppy is still whining and barking, then they are more than likely trying to get attention. Puppies love to be cuddled, and they are happiest when in the company of others. They will have to get used to being in their crate. Here are some tips on getting through the first night or two without losing sleep:

Take the puppy out for a walk, play ball, or perform some other type of vigorous exercise just before putting them to bed. Give them a good hour of exercise to burn off their energy.

Put him in the crate at least an hour before you plan to go to bed yourself. This gives him time to give up the whining before you are ready to sleep. Do not feed the puppy right before putting him in the crate. You want him to digest his food and poop before going into the crate.

A new puppy can be like a newborn baby. They may cry the first night or two, but they will get used to going to bed as long as they are well cared for before going down for the night.

6.2. CHEWING THE HOUSE

A teething puppy will chew anything and everything that they can get their little mouths around. If you have a large breed puppy that is growing quickly, you could have a big slobbery mouth chewing on your table legs, bedroom suit, and even your children's toys. As soon as you decide to bring a puppy into your home, you have to bring out the puppy toys to spare your home from becoming one big teething toy.

Ideally, you will already have your puppy under close supervision. Inappropriate chewing and gnawing become just one more thing that you have to watch out for and immediately correct. **Catching the puppy in action and redirecting his efforts** to something more appropriate is the most effective way to send the message that your home is not to be chewed.

Unfortunately, you have to redirect that attention away from the inappropriate chewing repeatedly until your puppy fully gets the message. A puppy only adjust his behavior if he has an alternative that he know is more appropriate and approved by you. This means that

you have to correct and redirect as soon as you notice he is chewing something and give him an alternative that is acceptable.

7. ONE WEEK PLAN

Here's a sample schedule that you can try to help create a routine for your puppy, and help him learn things with ease:

- Upon waking up, take the puppy to his potty place.
- After peeing and defecating, go for a brisk walk, and go ahead and play with the dog. You can try fetch or any other game that would require your dog to participate. Do this for around 10 minutes.
- Spend another 10 minutes as "quality time" for you and your puppy. Just pet and talk to him, and use this time to check if there is anything wrong with him, such as his coat, his attitude, his eyes, etc.
- Now, it's time for your puppy to eat! Give him fresh puppy chow, and make sure his water is fresh and clean, too.
- Bring the puppy out again to pee or defecate. This is inherent to them, especially after meals.
- If you're going to go to work, your puppy should take a nap. Or, you could play with him, or ask somebody else to do it.
- After the nap, play with the dog again or go out with him for a walk. Just give him time to enjoy his surroundings.

- If you're home, allow your puppy to watch you move around the house.
- Change your puppy's water, feed him, and play with him again. It's good to let him play until he gets tired so it would be easier for him to sleep.
- Now's the time for another "quality time" with your puppy. You could use it for grooming him, talking to him, or letting him watch TV or listen to music with you.
- Finally, before going to bed, bring your puppy to his potty place one more time.

However, it is important to note the following in your schedule:

- Puppies won't be able to sleep unless they've had enough opportunities to play and go to their potty place. Make sure that if you cannot be around with them the whole day, they have a lot of toys, other pets, or people to play with. Just like you, puppies really do not want to get bored, too. Puzzle or chew toys are helpful because they easily keep puppies preoccupied. The key here is that if the puppy was able to utilize his day well, he would not have a hard time sleeping at night— which will also be good for you!

- A comfortable environment. Don't expect puppies to enjoy time with you if your house looks like an entire mess. If you have an indoor puppy, it's always best to make sure that his surroundings are clean, and that there are no awful odors and that you're able to give him the kind of life that he deserves.

- Feed the puppy once or twice a day. There are some puppies who like to eat once every four to five hours, though, especially those from smaller breeds. The important thing is to make sure that your dog is properly fed so he wouldn't wake up hungry, or too full, in the middle of the night.

Puppies always need to be fed much more than dogs as they are still growing. Plus, always check your puppy's appetite. There are days when he'd want to eat more, and when there are times that he does not want to eat, maybe you should check if he's experiencing any illnesses or conditions.

- Eliminating is important. While dogs only need to do so at least once every 8 hours, puppies need to be let out more often since their bodies are only adjusting to a routine.

- Say a magic word. It's also good if you could provide your dog with a magic word that would help him realize it's time to sleep. For example bed, sleep, good night, sleep now, etc. It's important to say this every time he goes to bed, so he will associate the act of sleeping with it.

- Time is essential. And of course, make sure that you give your puppy ample amounts of time. Puppies need to feel comforted, and loved, and if you don't have enough time for them, why did you even get them in the first place? When a puppy is loved, he won't feel the need to ask for your attention especially in the middle of the night.

8. CONCLUSION

Puppy training can turn out to be a bit difficult effort, but hard work and persistence pay off. Remember that everything that seems like a simple process can become a tedious routine if not done correctly from the outset. As a novice, you may make avoidable mistakes when training your pup and this may be time-consuming, waste of energy and can be frustrating too. Not to mention that it can be confusing and scary for your little cute puppy.

Training your pup doesn't have to be hard, though. As a matter of fact, this book will make the whole process easy and stress-free, I hope this guide has simplified everything to do with puppy training. Common problems that many people run up against can be avoided just by knowing that they exist. Training your puppy does not have to be tedious and stressful, and with the right approach you will definitely find out it doesn't have to be.

Thank you for reading this book! Good luck in your training!

A STEP-BY-STEP program
so your pup will understand you!

POTTY
TRAINING

HOW TO POTTY TRAIN YOUR PUPPY
IN JUST 7 DAYS

ETHAN ADRIAN

INTRODUCTION

One of the biggest reasons puppies and dogs end up in shelters is because the owner has not been successful in-house training them. House training a puppy or dog is vital to your relationship, and it will ensure the two of you have a long and happy life together, free from the stress of messes in the house. The appropriate time to start potty training is as soon as you get your puppy because once a dog thinks it's okay for him to relieve himself in the house, it will become a difficult behavior to break.

As the owner, it's your responsibility to teach your puppy to mess outside. Puppies do not come equipped with this knowledge. If your puppy messes in the house, consider it your fault. You weren't watching him close enough! If he messes in his crate, consider that your fault as well! You left him in his crate too long. This may sound harsh but many problems could easily be avoided if puppies were better understood.

Before you bring your puppy home you need to be fully committed to the raising and training of your puppy. If you already have your puppy then you need to decide right now if you will commit yourself to properly train it. It takes time, patience, understanding, and persistence to train a well-behaved family companion.

But, I guarantee your hard work now will pay off with years of loving companionship.

Much like children you need to teach your puppy where and when it is acceptable to go to the bathroom. At the age of 12 weeks, puppies have little or no control over when and where they go. If your puppy is four months old they'll be able to wait around 4 hours to go potty. At night, by four months, your puppy should be able to hold it overnight. Establish a regular feeding schedule alongside your puppy out time and potty breaks.

When outside, try to take your puppy to a certain spot to go to the bathroom, this helps it associate inside and outside. Don't forget to praise your puppy when it does go potty in the right spot.

TIPS TO SUCCEED IN POTTY TRAINING

*T*hese are a few key tips that will help you achieve the desired behavior from your puppy when potty training him.

- **Maintain realistic expectations** - Even well-behaved puppies can be unpredictable on occasion. You're dealing with a very young dog, and changing behavior will take weeks and even months.
- **Remember affection works** - Puppies want to be loved, pet and rewarded. When you respond to positive behaviors with a lot of love, you have a much better chance of training your dog to behave. If you don't want your dog messing in the house, lead him outside to do his business. When he does it right and at the right spot, give him a treat and praise him.
- **Pay attention to your dog** - Not all puppies are exactly alike. They are unique, with different personalities and traits. What works for one puppy might not work for all puppies. The first few weeks that you spend with your puppy should tell you how he responds to certain

commands, consequences, and rewards. Instead of working against the puppy's natural instincts, work with them. It's important to train a puppy not to mess in the house rather ring the puppy doorbell or bark when he wants to go out to potty.

But you want the dog to have the freedom to bark when there is the danger, so it's important to balance behavior modification with remembering that a dog is going to be a dog. If your puppy barks excessively, don't get mad at or shout at him. The dog may get the impression that you too are joining in. Consistently say "**quiet**" in a firm and calm voice when you want him to stop barking. After he stops barking, take him out to potty and reward him with praise and a treat.

- **Keep your commands clear** - Tell your puppy exactly what you want. Saying "**no**" is a command, but if you want the puppy to do something beyond that, you need to be specific. Get a puppy to sit or lie down by physically pointing to or patting a spot where the dog should rest and remain. You don't want to confuse your puppy and if you're just yelling all the time, it's not going to dissuade bad behavior.
- **Maintain consistency** - Dogs learn from repetition. You'll need to practice behavior training with your puppy on a regular basis. Teach them to go outside when they need to potty. If the puppy relieves himself in the house, don't get mad at him. Rather, clean the mess and continue with the potty training schedule until the puppy gets that it is appropriate to only potty outside.
- **Reinforce good behavior** - You aren't going to get the behavior you want from your puppy unless you reinforce it. Use treats liberally while training your puppy because they work. Playing outside, taking walks and just cuddling on the couch are other positive reinforcements that will work with your dog. Don't hand out treats for no reason. Give

them to your puppy specifically after a good behavior is produced. When the dog stops messing in the house and goes outside to potty, reward that dog with a treat. It might seem like bribery, but that's okay. Your goal is to do what works.

Once your puppy has reached the right age, it's important to establish a potty training routine and to be consistent and patient with it. You will need to take your puppy out immediately after he wakes up, 15 minutes after he eats or drinks, at least once an hour while he is awake before you put him in his crate and immediately after you take him out of the crate. To help prevent accidents, be sure you keep your puppy on a regular feeding schedule and remove the food once he has finished eating, but always allow him access to water. Puppy's digestive systems are quick and efficient and taking him out 15 minutes after he eats will help get him used to go potty outside.

Puppies cannot be expected to hold their bladders all night, so you will also need to set an alarm during the night so you can take him outside. Expecting your puppy to hold his bladder throughout the night is not only unrealistic, it is a sure fire way to ensure he soils his crate or gets a nasty bladder infection trying to hold it far longer than he is capable of or should be expected. It is also important to watch for the bathroom "**tells**" puppies often display. Twirling in circles, whining, scratching and sniffing the floor are often indications the puppy needs to potty, so if you see or hear these things, take him outside immediately.

It is also important that you take your puppy to the same spot every time to use the bathroom. Be patient with your puppy, do not try to force him, yell at him or rush him to use the potty. Simply stand in the designated spot and use upbeat, positive verbal encouragements to "**go potty**" and allow your puppy time to sniff out the perfect spot and do his business. Once your puppy does his business, be sure to reward him with positive praise, a treat and lots of snuggles, pets, and kisses. Make it a rewarding, happy experience so your dog feels good when he sees you get the leash and say the words "**go potty**." Most puppies truly want to please their masters and letting your puppy know he is good and did the right thing will help your puppy's potty training progress at a faster rate.

HOW TO EFFECTIVE POTTY TRAIN A PUP

- **Journal keeping** – When potty training a pup, it is crucial that you understand how commonly your pup has to relieve himself. If your dog's routine is stable, he will normally have a constant washroom regimen. Tape-record exactly what time they went and what business they did. Determine how long they are holding it. That is your standard. It is necessary during this time that you feed your dog on a routine. Do not leave the bowl of kibble on the ground, or it will be difficult to predict accidents.
- **Crate** – a crate is a helpful tool when it comes to potty training a pup. Now that you have actually established a baseline with your journal, you know how long your dog can hold it.
- **Taking him out** - When you are house-training your dog, you must always go outside with him to see that he goes. Walk him (don't hold him) out the door you at some point desire him to use to alert you. This will build a routine. Once he does his business, wait a few more minutes. Many puppies will go again virtually instantly. You will learn your new puppy's regular. Any time he does his business outside, praise him and offers him a treat or fun game.
- **Create a routine** – After a successful first step in potty training pup, it is time to repeat the same after a scheduled period of time. Take him outside and await him to do the proper business. If he does, give him a reward and allow him house freedom.
- **Learn how to handle and prevent accidents** - Your dog must never be running free in the house without you. If you cannot supervise, put him in his pet crate. You can't penalize for mishaps after the truth because canines don't

74

discover that way. If you see him start to show the indications, such as smelling, turning in a circle or squatting, start clapping your hands and rush him out the marked door. Do not get upset, simply act urgently. As soon as he gets outside, rewards him for going.

The key thing to pup potty training is consistency. With the few tricks and techniques above, your pup will house break in just a short period of time.

POTTY TRAINING

*T*he most effective method to achieve quality results in potty training your puppy is using the clicker. **Clicker training** is a training method which relies on positive reinforcement, rather than coercion or correction, and uses the principles of both classical conditioning and operant conditioning. The Clicker Potty Training Method is designed for puppies and dogs of all breeds, ages, and sizes. **This method will work** no matter what your schedule is, provided you follow the guidelines. Before you begin this or any potty training method, keep in mind that young puppies just aren't capable of holding it for extended periods of time. Once they are anywhere from 3-5 months old they should be able to hold it for longer periods. Consult your vet if you feel your puppy is going way too much or not enough because some potty training problems are caused by the puppy or dog being ill.

Don't expect too much from your puppy either. He's a puppy and will do what comes naturally or what was unintentionally taught to him. It's your job to teach him what is and isn't acceptable behavior. Don't slack off because you feel your puppy is stupid and incapable of learning or because you've just had it with trying to teach him to go outside for three weeks and he's still messing in the house. All puppies can and will learn if given the proper instruction and time to learn. So get ready to begin properly potty training your puppy! Before we begin, take note of these potty training steps:

- Ensure that you take your puppy out when he wakes up, after eating and drinking, when you first get home, and after play sessions.
- Take him outside through the same door.
- Take him to the same spot.
- Bring him back in through the same door.
- Take your puppy out on a leash.
- Clean up messes inside with a solution of half vinegar and half water.
- Choose a phrase as his "**Go potty**" signal and use it as soon as you get him to his spot.
- Leave a few stools at his bathroom area.
- Rush your puppy outside if he starts to mess in the house.
- Keep him on a set schedule for feeding, walking.
- Learn not to rub your puppy's nose in his mess.
- Make sure you don't leave him in his crate for longer periods than he can handle.
- Avoid scolding or hitting him for making a mess in the house.
- Avoid playing with him before he goes to the bathroom.
- Don't allow let him run around the house before he's fully trustworthy.
- Avoid the use of newspaper when potty training. They're messy and confuse your pup.
- Make sure you do not use different doors to take him outside and back in.
- You should never ignore your puppy's need to go out no matter how tired you are.

This method is based on the popular clicker training for dogs. Instead of using the clicker for every aspect of training, you'll be using it for potty training only, thereby increasing its effectiveness. If you don't have a clicker, visit your nearest pet store. You should be able to get two of them for just a few dollars. Make sure you get two just in case you misplace or break one.

You can use this method whether you have a puppy or dog, work all day or are at home, or if you've already started a different potty training method and it hasn't worked. Simply throw out the other ideas you've had about potty training and start fresh. This method is so easy to teach and most puppies and dogs will catch on extremely quickly. Keep in mind though that **your puppy will need to have a good diet and a strict schedule**. No puppy will become potty trained if he is fed "**less than quality**" food and if he's fed whenever. You need to be completely dedicated, no matter how tired you are! Remember, a puppy learns only what he has been taught. Your puppy's good behavior, or lack of, reflects directly on you! Before you begin with this method you need to set your puppy up for success.

Since your puppy is young, chances are he simply can't hold it for more than a few hours at a time. It would be very cruel of us to expect him to hold it all day so be prepared to clean up messes until he's around 3-5 months of age. To help control where he messes in the house you will need to set up a room, an exercise pen, or a large crate. Any of these three will be large enough for him to have areas to play, sleep, and mess. If we don't give him room to do these things he will probably develop the nasty habit of messing where he sleeps. This is a very difficult habit to break so let's prevent it from ever happening. If you use a room or exercise pen I suggest having a crate available for him to sleep in. This will prepare him for when he's older and you want to crate him when you leave.

When you set up the area he will use when alone, be sure he has something comfortable to sleep on, and the material you want him to normally mess on outside. If you want him to always go on the grass, place a piece of sod in his area. One piece should last nearly a week if you just clean up the poop. You want to leave the urine smell in the sod since this will attract your puppy back to the sod. If you prefer he always go on the cement outside, get a thin slab of cement for his area.

Again, **just clean off the poop** and every few days rinse the slab with plain water. It is inappropriate to cover the floor with newspapers since this gets very messy and it teaches him to use any newspaper as his toilet. You'll also want to make sure he has some good toys to play with. You can also place a small dish of water in his area.

Now we're ready to begin! If you haven't brought your puppy home yet plan on starting this from the second you pick him up. If you already have your pup, start this when you'll have a few full days to work on it. First, we need to associate the clicker with something very good. There is no better reward for a puppy than a **tasty treat** when training.

And what behavior other than going to the bathroom outside deserves something this good? Grab your puppy, the clicker, and a few treats you know your puppy likes. It will work better if you do this outside on the surface you want him to use, at his designated potty spot, since you'll always be clicking and treating his behavior outside.

All you need to do now is **click a few times** then give him a treat. Choose how many times you'll click the clicker so he knows what he's doing well every time. Once or twice should do. Be sure to only give him a small piece of the treat. Don't give him a whole mouthful. Continue to click and treat every few minutes. Once he hears the clicks and looks to you for a treat you know he's caught on. Now we wait until he goes to the bathroom. As soon as he starts to pee or poop click the clicker, however, many times you've decided on. When he's finished, give him a treat and **really praise him**. Put your clicker away until the next time you take him out to the bathroom. Repeat this every time he goes.

Once your puppy has had no accidents in the house for at least 2 weeks, it's time to start teaching him to let you know when he needs to go out. This will be addressed in the upcoming section, The Puppy Doorbell. After teaching him how to let you know he needs to go out, it's **time to start eliminating the clicker and treats**. This should only be started after at least two weeks of no accidents in the house and your pup letting you know consistently that he needs to go out.

We can now assume that your puppy understands that he is expected to go to the bathroom outside and that he'll let you know it, so it should be safe to begin! Start this on a weekend morning or anytime you'll have a few days to dedicate to this.

Take him out as you normally would in the morning. Click and treat as normal for this time. The next time you take him out, don't click but give a treat. Couple this with plenty of praise. Take him back in and wait until the next time he needs to go out. Click and treat for this one. Do the click and treat for every other bathroom break for the rest of the day. If he seems okay with everything and is still going to the door to be let out, with no accidents in the house, we can move on to the next day. If he backslides even one time with either not letting you know he needs to go out or going to the bathroom in the house, go back to click and treating every time. He obviously isn't ready. Give him a few more days and try again. If everything went smoothly your first day, click and treat every third bathroom break. Continue this for a few days and if all is well, try eliminating the click and treat altogether for one day. If he has accidents in the house go back a step.

If all goes well, **forget the click and treat** for a few days and monitor his behavior. If he seems okay with the new arrangement, pat yourself on the back! You now have a potty trained puppy!

If your puppy makes a mistake in the house, go back one step and continue working on that particular step for a few days. Some puppies may catch on to this right away and others may take weeks or even months. But I assure you that this method is by far easier to teach than any other method. Puppies just seem to understand what is expected of them better than strictly using a crate or exercise pen. Keep in mind that **you shouldn't use the clicker for any other training**. You don't want to confuse him.

You can alter this method to fit your needs for other potty training. If you want to train your pup to mess in a litter box, simply click every time he goes in it. Follow the same guidelines, with the exception of teaching him how to let you know he needs to go out. Or if you have a doggy door, you can teach this method with much quicker results. Set your pup's pen up in front of the doggy door when you're gone and he'll be potty trained in no time! First, you must teach him to go out the doggy door. This is a matter of simply coaxing him through it, while you hold it open, to get his dinner. Do this a few times until he seems okay with it. Then close the door and have someone coax him through to the other side. This shouldn't take much more than a few times. When teaching with the use of a doggy door keep in mind that you'll still need to go out with him to click and treat. Let him go out the doggy door and once he's through you simply go out behind him.

FOR TWO PUPPY HOMES

Potty training using a clicker for more than one puppy can be **a little tricky**. You don't want one puppy to hear the click from outside and think he's done something good inside. This could very well turn out disastrous! At the same time, potty training could go much quicker. I assume you'll be taking both of the puppies outside at the same time? When one puppy goes, click and treat him. The other one will want a treat too so wait until he goes then click and treat him. **Puppies are very competitive** so once your pups catch on that they'll get a treat for going outside they'll be trying to go quicker than the other one so they get the treat first! If you're having trouble with them only wanting to play while they're supposed to be going to the bathroom, you'll have to take them out one after the other

Hopefully, each of their potty areas is in an area where the pup inside won't hear the clicker. Close the window if you think he'll hear. Once they catch on that going to the bathroom brings a click, which produces a treat, they'll be much more apt to go when taken out together. Make sure they each have their own bathroom area, too. It doesn't need to be on opposite sides of the yard but rather 5-10 feet apart.

THE PUPPY DOORBELL

Everyone wants their puppy to notify them when he needs to go out. You'll have to decide how you want your pup to let you know. Most people don't want their pup jumping on the door or scratching at the door since this only creates damaged doors. The easiest method I've taught to date is **the puppy door bell**. You simply hang a bell from your doorknob, mount it on the wall at your pup's level, or use one of those bells that you hit the top and it dings (place this kind on the floor). Or you can use another method of teaching your puppy to bark when he needs to go out. I find this method much more difficult to teach since many puppies won't bark until they're older, and some breeds just aren't inclined to bark. I'm going to teach you how to teach your puppy to notify you of the use of a bell.

Before you can work on this, though, your puppy needs to know that messing is supposed to be done outside only. Your **puppy should be fully trustworthy** when you're home with him in the house. It works best at this time because your puppy knows he should go outside, but he just doesn't know how to get out. And at this time, he should be old enough to hold it for longer periods, allowing you to take him out at certain times without having to clean up any messes in the house.

Once you've got your bell in place, you'll need to show your puppy the bell. Encourage him to sniff it, lick it, whatever. If he happens to make it sound off open the door and take him out. If he doesn't make it sound off, you can do it, then open the door and take him out. I suggest having his leash on him when you practice with the bell so you have control of him when you take him out. Of course, every time he does something good be sure to praise him; whether he touches the bell, makes it sound off, looks at the door after making noise, anything. Be most lavish with your praise if he rings the bell then looks to the door.

Have him ring the bell every time before you go out and very soon he should catch on that ringing the bell opens the door which allows him to go to the bathroom. Be very vigilant about this and before too long you will hear the bell when you're watching television. This is the time when you really praise and let him know how good he is. Immediately take him outside to his spot.

HOW TO HANDLE ACCIDENTS

*N*ow you're probably wondering **how to handle it** when he goes on and messes in the house. Well, you do nothing but clean it up. Don't scold him, yell at him, and never hit him. You **should not punish the puppy** for having an accident. Often times, this is going to do more harm than it will do good, and it can damage the trust that the puppy has built up for you, causing it to fear you. Simply ensure that you clean the area, making sure that the scent of the urine or feces is completely gone. This is important because if the puppy smells the scent, he will go back to the same area over and over again. At no point should you rub the puppy's nose in the urine or feces, as this could cause the dog to become very sick.

Greet him like you always do. If he goes in the house when he's loose and with you, consider it your fault. You simply weren't watching him close enough! Provided you click and treat every time he goes to the bathroom outside he will catch on that good things happen when he goes outside but nothing happens when he goes in the house. Before long, he'll want to go outside all the time to go to the bathroom and get a treat.

By using a few days to get him used to his spot outside on the surface you've chosen, chances are he'll go on that same surface in the house. If he doesn't, try making his indoor mess area a little bigger or placing a small chunk of sod where he's previously gone pee on top of his indoor sod. Before long, you should have a puppy that willingly holds it until he can get outside. **Don't expect too much** from a puppy under 12-16 weeks old or a small breed puppy, though. Young and very small puppies just aren't physically capable of holding it that long.

It is important to keep an eye on the puppy when you are potty training him. Do not allow him to have access to the entire house because this will raise the chance of him soiling in a hidden area when he's out of your line of sight. Keep doors to bedrooms closed and use dog gates to keep your pup within your line of vision at all times. It's important to remember that even the smartest puppies don't have bladder control yet. **Puppies younger than 12 weeks old** can't be trained yet because they just don't have the capability. Young dogs also don't know how to tell you when they need to eliminate their waste. They may be aware of it, but they have not yet figured out how to tell you.

Accidents are going to happen. Just accept accidents as part of the process and do not overreact to them. There are going to be times when the puppy simply has an accident, even though you have taken him outside regularly. Your puppy is not being willful, disobedient or resistant, it's simply part of the process so do not punish him by spanking him, rubbing his nose in it or yelling at him. If you notice your pup is beginning to pee or poop in the house, clap your hands or make a loud noise. You want to startle the puppy and get its attention, but you don't want to scare the dog. Calmly say "**No**" and take him to his spot outside.

You can also make a loud noise with the intention of startling the dog. For example, saying loudly, "**Outside**," and then take the puppy straight to his potty spot, and allow him to finish there. **Praise him** with a treat when he'd done.

When an accident does occur in the house, simply clean up the accident and move on. You cannot apply a correction after the fact, the puppy will have no idea what is going on, why he is being told

"**No**" or what it is he was supposed to do. If the puppy has frequent accidents, you might want to start taking it outside more often, because you do not want it to get confused and think it is okay for him to relieve himself inside of the house.

It is also **important for you to make plans** if you are going to be away from the house for a long period of time. It is very difficult for a person to house train a dog when they are at work 10 hours per day and the puppy is left alone all day. If this is going to be the case, have someone stay at your house, and **follow the puppy's schedule**.

Unlike humans, puppies live in the moment and once it has passed, they do not have a recollection of the accident and trying to discipline a puppy for a past action will only make him scared and make it difficult for him to trust you. Never, ever strike your puppy when you find accidents, or for any other reason. Hitting your puppy will only crush his spirit and break the bond you are trying to build; it will not correct his behavior or make the process faster.

Be patient and consistent with your potty training routine and be gentle, kind and loving with your puppy. You'd never yell at, punish or berate a baby for accidents, so don't do it to your puppy. Follow these potty training tips and in just a few weeks, your puppy will be potty trained and you can feel good about a job well done.

REGULAR FEEDING

*O*ne of the causes of puppies being sick and having irregular potty patterns or diarrhea is the food you feed your puppy and how you feed him. It is important that you make sure you feed your puppy on a regular schedule. Depending on the age of the puppy, he will **need to eat between three and four times each day**. If you feed your puppy on a schedule, it is more likely he will need to relieve himself at the same time each day, which will make house training much easier for the both of you.

You need to feed your puppy a **high-quality food**, which is more easily digested and that means fewer messes. And, contrary to what you've been told, puppies do not need fresh water available at all times. Leaving a large amount of **fresh water** out for your puppy just means more pee to clean up. Give him water before and after he eats and offers it throughout the day. If it's a hot day you'll need to give him more if he's outside for any length of time. Use your best judgment on this. If you feel he isn't getting enough water, offer him a little more. If you have your puppy outside for some time you will need to have fresh water available at all times.

Always feed your puppy at the same time every day. This will get his digestive system on a set schedule so you'll have a better idea of when he needs to go out. And whatever you do, don't change his normal food! Decide what food you want to feed him and stick with it. Puppies can easily get diarrhea if their food is changed. Try hard not to give him tons of treats throughout the day. For now, stick with just giving him treats for messing outside. **Walk your puppy at the same time** every day, too. Puppies get used to certain things and will come to expect them at the time they are used to.

You should also make sure you are picking up the puppy's food and water bowl at least two and a half hours before going to bed. This will help ensure the puppy does not eat too close to bedtime or in the middle of the night, which will help ensure the puppy does not relieve himself in the house while everyone is asleep.

Most puppies will be able to sleep for about seven hours without having to be taken outside. The puppy may, however, wake up in the middle of the night and need to relieve himself. Remain as quiet and calm as possible if this happens. First, do not turn on all of the lights in the house, but turn on as few as you can. Next, do not talk to the puppy or pet him, simply take him out, tell him to go potty, reward him when he is finished, and bring him back inside. If you talk to him, he is likely to think it is time to get up and play, which means he will not go back to sleep when you return indoors.

PUPPY NUTRITION

As discussed earlier in the previous chapters, puppy ownership entails a lot of care and much responsibilities. What to feed and how to do it, will be the first question that will come to your mind after bringing him home? Which food will be suitable food for your pup for the first few weeks or a month? Food with proper nutrient composition is needed for muscle development, organs, and strong bones.

However, it best recommended **to consult a veterinarian** first before embarking on any food program. With the rapid growth of the pup, there is need to keep on changing the food quality for his better health. Therefore, when it comes to feeding puppies, special care needs to be taken. It's important to ensure that certain essential nutrients are included in their diet to promote the healthy growth of bones, nervous system and coat. Due to their fragile digestive systems, try to give him the same food he ate before coming to your house. Gradually, over a one-week transition period, you can mix the old and new food.

Any food you purchase should be able to state in the labels the life stage for which the food is most suited for. If any food is labeled for **"growth"** or **"for all stages of life"**, it is probably a good food choice for your puppy.

It is time to access your puppy after feeding him a particular food for 6 weeks. If he is playful and energetic with a thick shiny coat, then he is probably digesting all his nutrients and there are no causes for alarm.

Know the right way to feed the puppy

Puppies that are not 6 months old yet should be fed thrice a day. After they reach 6 months old, it is okay **to feed them twice a day**. It is important to take advantage of the feeding guides provided on the labels on the puppy food. You should vary the amount of food you give your puppy every week ensuring the puppy is in a healthy and playful condition. Puppies require a lot of calories as they are still growing. Therefore it is important to check out your puppy's expected body size when you purchase him, so as to ensure he is eating the right food for his growth.

Some largely bred dogs develop skeletal and joint problems as they grow. This caused by the lack of certain nutrients that support growth in the largely bred dogs. The conditions can worsen if the puppy is overfed. It is important to take care when purchasing puppy food and be certain that the food will be of great benefit to the puppy in terms of growth and health. Foods meant for larger breeds tend to be low in calcium but high in fiber as they are designed to control the growth of the puppy.

How to discern the right kind of food

With the ever growing dog food industry, there are unlimited varieties and alternative of food that you can choose for your puppy. There are three main dog food that is dry food, wet food and dry food that can be served wet. You can opt for the best brand or go for a generic food if you are planning on saving money. The following factors are important in helping you choose the best food for your puppy:

- **Cost** - in the market, wet food is generally more expensive than dry food. Your choice of food will depend on your budget.
- **Nutrients** - In terms of nutrition, the dry food is the best

option. This is because the dry food takes a longer time to digest, unlike wet food that passes through the puppy very quickly. Wet food will not allow the puppy to absorb most of the nutrients due to the short time it takes in the digestion system of the puppy.

- **Storage** - Another determinant is the shelf life and storage of the dog food. Dry food is easily stored in a container with a lid. The dry food has a longer shelf life and can be stored for several months. On the other hand, wet food is hard to store and once opened it has a shorter shelf life and goes bad after a short period. Thus the storage and shelf life of the puppy food will play a big role in determining the best food for your puppy.
- **Dental Health** - The dental health of your puppy is determined by the food you give him. Experts recommend feeding your puppy dry food, apart from the fact that it makes it easy for potty training; dry food does not get trapped in the puppy's teeth. Wet food gets trapped in the puppy teeth and these may encourage bacterial infection causing the teeth to decay and unpleasant smell from your puppy's mouth.

It is **much healthier** for your puppy if you fed him either wet food or dry food. Avoid going for the moist food which has nutritional imbalance and high level of preservatives especially salt which may affect the health of your puppy negatively. You can also alternate between dry and wet food when feeding your puppy. For example, a meal of wet food can be followed by two meals of dry food can prove beneficial with a high amount of nutrients. However, it is advisable to ask the vet about the best combination for your puppy.

For the brand of puppy food, is good to go for **the most reputable brand** with the best nutrients for your puppy. The brand choice is also determined by the pricing and whether it is natural or generic.

CREATING A ROUTINE

*T*he most important step in potty training a dog is to create a schedule. Puppies and dogs do best when they follow a routine. Having a schedule teaches the dog that there are specific times for him to do specific activities. For example, there is a specific time for him to eat, there is a specific time each day for him to go for a walk and there are specific times each day for him to be taken outside to relieve himself. Most puppies can hold their bladder for 1 hour for every month of their age. This means that if the puppy is three months old, he can hold his bladder for three hours, however, you should never make him hold it for any amount of time longer than that.

Begin by taking your puppy outside **at least every two hours**. You will also want to take the puppy outside as soon as he wakes up in the morning, before bed at night, after play time, as well as after he has had something to eat or drink.

It is important to pick a place outside for your dog's bathroom area. This is because you do not want the dog going all over the yard, and you want to build a routine with him. Lead the dog to the area on his leash and say something like, "**Go potty**." After he has relieved himself, **give him praise**. You can also take him for a walk, or spend a few minutes playing with him to reinforce this behavior.

You can give your puppy a treat after he has relieved himself outside, but you have to remember to do this while you are still outside, and not once you have gone back into the house. You should also make sure the puppy is completely finished relieving himself before you give him the treat. This is because it is very easy for a puppy to become distracted, and if this happens, the puppy may forget he was not done and then remember once he is back inside of the house.

DAILY ROUTINE

Routine will make the puppy feel secure and will result in faster potty training. A sample daily routine looks like this and can easily be adjusted to fit any family's schedule:

7:00 am – 7:30 am

Wake up and go for a walk. Provide some playtime with the opportunity for the puppy to do his business.

7:30 am – 8:00 am

Feed the puppy breakfast in his crate. It is appropriate to feed on a Kong or other interactive item so the puppy learns to chew appropriate items, to stretch meal time out and have them eat slowly and to occupy the puppy for a period of time.

8:00 am – 9:00 am

After eating, give the puppy an outdoor opportunity to relieve himself.

9:00 am – 12:00 pm

The puppy might nap for a bit and then you can spend some time with him. You should give puppies the opportunity to do their business outside as soon as they wake up and after playtimes so they quickly learn to potty outside.

Puppy can go out for a walk with you.

Have a short (no more than 5 minutes) training session with rewards. Dogs learn quickly when they have frequent but short (less than 5 minutes) training sessions throughout the day.

12:00 pm – 1:00 pm

Take the puppy outside for a potty break, and then have a gentle playtime outside if the weather permits. Provide a meal in a Kong, puppies up to 16 weeks should have three meals a day. Then, 15 minutes after the puppy has finished eating, provide another potty opportunity outside.

1:00 pm – 5:00 pm

Give the puppy the opportunity to nap if he would like to. When he wakes, take him outside to do his business and then have a gentle playtime. Provide an opportunity for the puppy to nap again.

5:00 pm – 6:00 pm

Take the puppy outside for a break. Then take the puppy for a walk, and have a playtime and a short training session. It is important to play with your puppy as this is a bond building relationship opportunity and it creates rewards other than treats.

6:00 pm

Dinner with a Kong filled with the puppy's food or another interactive food dispensing toy.

6:15 pm or 6:30 pm

Bathroom break

7:30 pm – 10:00 pm

This is a good opportunity to brush and groom your dog, gently brush his teeth, and do quiet activities. Have a short evening walk.

Before Bedtime

Give the puppy another opportunity to go out and do their business one last time. After any activity, give the puppy an opportunity to relieve herself outside.

Remember all interactions with puppies are learning opportunities, so manage the interactions so the puppy is learning the right things and therefore enjoying learning.

CONCLUSION

It is both an amazing feeling and experience to have a well behaved energetic dog. However to achieve such a result you have to work and concentrate on your puppy so that when he grows, he is everything you expected. Potty training a puppy is one of the most difficult behavior training for a puppy owner. It takes a lot of patience and commitment to have a well potty trained puppy. So if you are thinking of getting a puppy or ready have one, get ready to get dirty when potty training him so that you can have a tidy dog in the future. Raise him like one of your own and make the bond grow stronger each day. It is important to be optimistic and slow to anger when you find or unfortunately, step on his poop or pee on. After reading this book to the last full stop, you will be able to potty train your puppy like a professional trainer and reap the benefits of having both a clean house and puppy.

Crate Training

How To Crate Train Your Puppy In Just 3 Days A Step-By-Step Program So Your Pup Will Understand You!

Ethan Adrian

INTRODUCTION

Crate training a dog can be a time consuming and demanding task, but once completed it will provide a lot of conveniences and will prove to be handy in different situations. Bringing home a dog or dog means that you have to shoulder the responsibility of having to train him so that he knows where to eliminate and which parts of the home he can access and which he cannot. Teaching a dog the house rules is one of the best ways to enjoy their company and it will also help him learn what he can chew upon and what things are not to be chewed upon.

Crates are also safe for transporting the pet in a car and they are also a good means of taking him to places where he can enjoy himself, especially in those places where dogs are not allowed to roam about freely. Proper crate training a dog will pay rich dividends and the crate in turn also can become a safe place where the pet can learn to spend their time happily. Just make sure that while confining him to the crate that he is also provided an adequate amount of drinking water. For this purpose, spill proof water bowls are the preferred choice or you can pick bowls that can be attached to the kennel gate.

It is important to select a suitable crate which ideally should be made of plastic or which are collapsible and made out of metal.

Collapsible kennels are good for a pet when the owner is going to be present in the home for long periods of time, but are not recommended if the owner is going to leave the pet unattended for long periods of time. Crates are available in a variety of size and are readily available at almost every pet store. The crate must however, be sufficiently large to contain the pet and it should be big enough to allow for him to stand and turn around freely.

The actual crate training a dog process can last for a day or it can extend to weeks. The duration taken to complete crate training of your pet depends on factors such as the age and temperament of your dog as well as your own experience in training dogs. What is important is that you should ensure that the crate reminds the dog of something pleasant and the training must be performed in small steps that are to be taken one at a time.

To start the crate training process, you will first of all have to introduce the pet to his crate. It helps if you place the crate in an area that sees much human activity. In addition, it also helps to place a soft towel or blanket in the crate after which you can introduce your pet to his crate and be sure to use a soothing tone of voice when telling him to enter the crate. Be careful that the door to the crate is left open and fastened in that position to prevent it from accidentally closing and hitting the dog which will cause him to be frightened and even injured.

You can use some small treats which can be placed in the crate. Doing this will encourage your pet to enter and use the crate. Do not try forcing your pet into entering the crate, but instead cajole him and induce him with some treats in a bid to get him to enter into the crate.

Next, be sure to feed him his meals in his crate. This is an important step that should be taken after the pet has been introduced to his crate. Then, get him to stand comfortably in his crate and allow him to eat his meals there but close the crate door while he is doing this. Follow this up by opening the door as soon as he has finished eating his meal and then leave the crate door open, but ensure that he remains in his crate. Once he gets used to staying in the crate, you can start to condition him to remain in the crate for extended periods of time.

Once he has got into the habit of eating his meals in his crate and he does not show any fear or anxiety at being left in his crate, you can allow him to remain there for a short while, but under your supervision. You can start calling him over to his crate and by giving him a treat; you can get him to enter his crate.

Encourage him to get into his crate by either using commands or by pointing to the inside of the crate and give him a treat once he follows your instructions. Once in, you should praise your pet and give him another treat after which it is safe to shut the crate door. All that remains in so far as crate training a dog goes is to then stay with him for about ten minutes and then leave him in his crate for a few minutes in your absence. Then, return to the crate , open its door and let him out.

CHAPTER 1. BENEFITS OF CRATE TRAINING PUPPIES

*A*lmost all dogs are crated for one reason or another at some time in their lives. Either at the vets, in kennels, at a hotel when on holiday or for traveling by air. So whether you plan to regularly use a crate at home or not, many of the benefits of crate training a dog or dog still apply. Dog crates are such an incredibly useful tool to use in management, training and as a safety device for your dog that I strongly recommend you do use one and crate train your Golden Retriever properly to accept and even love their crate.

The following article discusses the many benefits both you and your Golden can enjoy the use of a crate.

It Speeds Up The House Training Process

Puppies are born with a strong denning instinct inherited from their distant ancestors to keep the place in which they den, the place they eat and sleep while a dog, clean of urine and feces. A crafty dog owner can use this knowledge to massively decrease the amount of time required to housebreak a dog and avoid many of the little accidents they have to clean up in the process. When you place your dog in the crate, they will refrain from going to the toilet there as long as they possibly can.

Stop Destructive Chewing And Nurture Chew Toy Habits

Golden Retrievers chew as dog's, as adolescents and most as adults too! It's a common trait for the breed that comes from their working retriever genes and you will not be able to prevent it. So to save your house and belongings, you need to teach them what they can and can't chew and an important part of this is preventing bad habits from forming. When you're supervising and catch them chewing something they shouldn't, you can redirect them to chew something that's allowed. But if you can't watch them you should put them in their crate with acceptable chew toys. This accomplishes two things:

It prevents them from being able to chew the wrong things and so prevents bad habits forming.

They spend much more time chewing on the correct toys you do want them to chew on and they form strong habits and addictions to these. The result? Less or no chewing on the things they shouldn't and an addiction to chewing on the things that they should.

A Crate Keeps Your Dog Safe When You're Unable To Watch Them

If you cannot supervise your dog or dog there is so much opportunity for them to get into mischief. And mischief could mean some expensive damage to your belongings or put themselves into a dangerous situation. Every year thousands upon thousands of dogs need medical treatment for eating poisonous substances, chewing electrical wiring or swallowing man-made objects. If you cannot supervise them and jump in if they start to get into trouble, you can prevent these things happening by crating them a short while.

A Crate Gives A Dog Feelings of Safety and Security

One of the major benefits of crate training a dog is they learn to see it as their own special little place where they can go to feel safe and secure. Many dogs in modern life find it very hard to get away from things, with busy households, kids running around and most likely other pets.

A Crate Is A Good Management Tool To Use When Solving Behavior Problems

There's usually a two-prong approach to solving any behavior problems that do develop, training and management. The training part is where you actively work on teaching a new behavior in place of the problem behavior you'd like to stop. The management part is your attempts to prevent your dog having the opportunity to perform the problem behaviors at all. This combination of preventing your dog performing the behavior and getting away with it, as well as training a new one gradually cures the behavior problem.

A Crate Is Used For Time Outs And Calming Your Dog

A crate is a useful tool for timeouts if you ever need to take your dog out of an environment to calm them down when over-excited and cannot be controlled. This often happens when they've been playing with another dog or dog , young children, or even a vigorous game of tug with yourself. A dog can often become so aroused and over-excited that it's very hard if not impossible to calm them down again. Sometimes a time out is the only option.

So you can place them in a crate for a couple of minutes until they've calmed themselves down and can then be let back out.

CHAPTER 2. CHOOSING THE BEST TYPE OF CRATE FOR YOUR DOG

So you have decided to get a pet crate for your dog and now you are faced with the *q*uestion of what type to get. Maybe you are not even sure what types of dog crates are out there. To answer your *q*uestions about crate types and the best one for your situation, I will give you a short review of each here.

The two main types of dog crates are wire and plastic. Plastic crates are also known as carriers and are made of molded two-piece units with ventilation and a door at the front. Wire crates are made from welded metal panels that are hinged together. There are pros and cons for each type; I will discuss the critical ones here.

Plastic and wire crates are both recommended for house-training

CHAPTER 2. CHOOSING THE BEST TYPE OF CRATE FOR YOUR DOG

and both are effective. Which one you choose depends on your own needs and preferences. Plastic pet crates are more den-like because they are more enclosed and private, although you may modify a wire crate to be more enclosed by covering it with a towel/blanket or purchasing a cover set for it. Plastic crates typically meet airline requirements for shipping your pet, whereas wire crates do not. Also, plastic crates are generally less expensive than wire crates. However, plastic crates are susceptible to chewing and are bulky to store. Wire crates are completely collapsible making them easy to store in small spaces. The openness of wire crates also allows for your pet to see all around him and provides better ventilation for snub-nosed dogs that may have trouble breathing in a plastic crate. Both types of dog crates come in a variety of sizes to accommodate any breed of dog, from a tiny Toy Poodle to a huge Great Dane, so your selection depends on your preference and needs, both now and in the future.

Some other types of dog crates that are available include soft-side, wicker, and wood or end table crates. These types of pet crates are not recommended for training purposes but instead provide a more attractive alternative for the mature and trained dog. These also come in a variety of sizes, although extreme sizes may be more limited. Soft-sided crates are excellent choices for someone on-the-go as they are simple to break-down and set-up. Wicker and wood crates offer a more attractive option than the standard wire or plastic crate. Again, these are not training crates but are a desirable option for the dog owner who wishes to purchase a crate for their dog but also wants something that complements the decor of the room that it will be set up in.

Ultimately, your best bet when selecting a dog crate is to determine your specific needs and preferences and then do some shopping around.

Crate Training a Puppy - Avoid These Common Mistakes

The last thing you ever want to do when crate training your puppy is using the crate for discipline. This defeats the whole purpose of crate training. You want your dog to feel safe, secure and happy in the crate. You want your dog to willingly go into the crate when he wants to. Forcing your puppy inside the crate will not help him get over his anxiety. Forcing your puppy inside will only make crate training harder. By yelling at your dog, scolding, shoving your dog inside out of spite will not help your dog's transition into the crate a smooth one (if one at all.)

Remember to slowly introduce the crate to your dog. Your dog is going to feel uneasy at first, do your best to associate good things with his crate. Put treats and toys in his crate and make sure you give him a lot of praise and rewards when he progresses.

Too Much Time in the Crate?

Remember, you're dealing with a young animal here. Like children, puppies can only hold their bladder for so long. This means if you work an 8-hour job and your puppy is in his crate all day, be expected to come home to a soiled crate. Generally speaking, for every month your puppy is old, is to how many hours plus one your new puppy can hold his bladder. For example, if your puppy is 2 months old, he can hold his bladder for 3 hours. If your puppy is 5 months old, he can only hold his bladder for 6 hours.

Expecting your dog to not soil his crate is unrealistic and unfair. Dogs instinctively hate to soil their sleeping areas, so your dog will do his best to hold his bladder and bowels, the least you can do is come home on your lunch break and take him out for a walk as well as feed him and give him water. With that said, avoid putting food and water in your dog's crate to prevent accidents.

You may think it's cruel but not coming home every few hours when your puppy needs you is even crueler. You need to take your dog outside frequently throughout the night if you don't want him to urinate in his crate. Also, the crate is only used whenever you're not home or at night to sleep. Down the road, you will eventually keep his crate open and he can come and go as he pleases.

Puppy Crate Training at Night

To prevent any night-time accidents (especially in your bed) avoid allowing your puppy sleep with you in your bed. At night, put your dog in his crate and cover up his crate with a blanket. The blanket will help keep your dog from seeing you and keep him calm, pretty similar to "out of sight, out of mind."

Use an old blanket in case your puppy chew or pulls apart the blanket from the inside of his crate. If your puppy is whining at night and it's driving you nuts, your best bet would be to put your dog and his crate in another room. Don't forget to take your dog out a couple times at night and immediately come morning.

These are the biggest mistakes people make when crate training their dog. Make sure you avoid any of these mistakes to get the best out of crate training.

CHAPTER 3. HOW TO START CRATE TRAINING A DOG

The dog crate is a useful, and sometimes life saving tool. You recently acquired a new family member, whether a dog or an adult dog, and a process of adjustment and learning the rules of your household begins.

Tips Before You Start Crate Training

Consistency: I can't stress this enough. Be Consistent. Do the same things, make the same gestures, and say the same words all the time and your dog will learn faster as a result.

Patience: To lose patience with your new dog is to take 2 steps backward in any training process. Always keep in mind that if you stay calm, your dog will stay calm too, which in turn will generate confidence and trust.

Personality: Each dog learns differently, which can lengthen or shorten the success of the crate training process, or any training exercise for that matter. Dogs have personalities that are as variable as humans and we have to adjust accordingly.

DOG CRATE TRAINING PROCESS

1. INTRODUCE YOUR DOG TO HIS CRATE

*B*ring the crate to the room you spend the most time in. Put a soft blanket in the crate. Sit down beside the crate, propping the door open with your body so it won't swing and scare your dog. You may even want to remove the door at the beginning. Call your dog in a sing-song, happy voice. You may even incorporate the "come" command at this point. Reward your dog with a treat, and then put a treat on the floor in front of the crate, one on the ledge, and a couple inside the crate. If your dog hesitates and backs up, that's okay, do not try to coax him. Leave the treats and walk away. You may have to repeat this process a few times. If food or treats are not an enticement, try a toy. If your dog runs into the crate to retrieve a ball, it was his idea to enter. The outcome of this exercise is to make your dog believe it was his choice to walk into the crate, not yours.

2. Eating Meals in the Dog Crate

Once your dog will walk in and out of the crate on his own, you can start feeding him his meals inside. At first leave the door open while he is eating, giving him quiet praise. When you feel the time is right, have him enter his crate, put the food down, praise him, and shut the door. When he has finished eating, immediately open the door. If he is comfortable with the door being closed, slowly lengthen the time before you open the door after he is finished eating. If he starts to whine, you may have increased the length of time too quickly. This is a critical point. You cannot let him out before he stops whining, otherwise, he will then associate whining to being let out of his crate. Wait until he is quiet, and then let him out. At his next feeding, cut back the time and proceed from there.

3. Lengthening Your Dog's Crate Time

Now that our dog is eating his meals and staying in his crate comfortably and without anxiety, you can crate him for short periods of time other than his feeding time. Call him in your sing-song voice, point inside the crate with a treat and/or toy in your hand, and close the door, leaving the treat or toy inside with him. Sit in the same room for a short time, get up and leave the room for about 30 minutes, then come back and sit in the same room for 5 to 10 minutes. If your dog is quiet, let him out of his crate and praise him. Repeat this process until you feel your dog is relaxed and content to be left in his crate while you are out of the room. Work your way up to a couple of hours of crate time without your presence. Depending on your dog's personality and energy level this part of dog crate training could take up to a couple of weeks. If your dog makes a fuss while you are out of the room the first time, ignore him and do not let him out until he settles down and is quiet.

4. Crating Your Dog During the Day

Your dog is now happily spending 30 minutes to 2 hours in his crate while you exit the room. The next step is to leave him in his crate while you make a short trip away from home. For this exercise you use your command and point to the crate, giving him a treat and a toy to play with. The treat could be optional at this point. Vary your routine when you are getting ready to leave and crate him anywhere from 5 to 20 minutes before stepping out the door. Make this a matter-of-fact exercise and refrain from any prolonged good-byes. Crate him, treat him and walk out the door. When you return home, come in quietly and keep your arrival low-key. Your dog will be enthusiastic to see you but do not reward him for his excited behavior by responding in kind. Let him out of his dog crate after he has calmed down and you are settled. Continue to feed him in his crate and reinforce crate time now and again for 30 minutes just so he doesn't relate crate time with you leaving him alone.

5. Crating Your Dog During the Night

Put your dog in his crate in the usual manner. You may want to have the crate in the bedroom or hallway near your bedroom door. If you have a dog , the bedroom is the best place during the night as they tend to need a potty break in the wee hours and you will be able to hear him if he whines to get out. Adult dogs sometimes prefer to sleep near you as they feel socially isolated in another part of your home. If you prefer the dog crate be somewhere else in your home, wait until your dog sleeps through the night and then slowly move the crate to where you prefer it to be.

6. Utilizing the crate

If you're going to be busy for a while and can't keep an eye on your pup, place him outside if you have a fenced area. If not, place him in his crate. Give him a toy or two to play with and keep him busy. Don't keep him in the crate for more than a couple of hours though. It's not a kennel. If you start confining him to the crate for most of the day and night, he will think of it as a cage, not a den. Going to the store for a couple hours? Repeat the process with your pup-tire him out, take him to relieve himself and place him in his crate with some toys.

When you get home, calmly take him outside. Eventually, as your pup gets used to the routine, you can crate him for half a day while you attend to work or shopping or other things. If you are going to be gone for longer than 3 or 4 hours, arrange for someone to come let your pup out and play with him during the mid-day break. As your pup matures (at about 5 or 6 months) you can leave him in the crate while you're at work all day. If you have a fenced backyard, it's preferable to leave him there, with plenty of water. If this is not an option, you can place him in his crate with a small bowl of water (like the kind rabbit cages have that attach to the mesh gate). Give him toys to chew on and amuse himself with.

CHAPTER 4. HOW TO CRATE TRAIN YOUR DOG: THE WEEKEND PLAN

Some trainers and behaviorists recommend introducing your dog to a new crate very gradually, over a period of a week or more. This method works well for timid dogs who fear confinement and for dogs who have already learned to dislike crates. But many dogs can learn to use crates more easily, and many people just don't have the time to devote an entire week or more to training before being able to use a crate.

If you need to start using a crate as soon as possible, try the following Weekend Crate Training plan. After your training sessions on Saturday and Sunday, you'll be able to start confining your dog in her crate on Monday.

To successfully use this crate - training plan, you'll need to follow the directions below, step by step. It's important to avoid skipping ahead and leaving your dog alone in the crate before she's ready. To confine your dog at night over the weekend, put her in a small, safe area instead. You can use an exercise pen or baby gate to block off part of your kitchen, a bathroom or a laundry room. Make sure that the area is dog - proofed and free of things that your dog shouldn't chew. You can leave her with something comfy to lie on, some water, her toys and some chew things to keep her occupied. It's best not to leave your dog home alone at all during the day on Saturday or Sunday. If you must do so for some reason, you can use the same dog - proofed area so as not to deviate from your training plan.

PREPARATION

CHOOSING A CRATE

*P*et supply stores and online vendors sell wire crates, plastic airline crates and mesh crates. Each style has its own advantages. Wire crates usually collapse for easy storage and portability, and they provide more ventilation than plastic ones. Plastic crates seem especially den - like and might make dogs feel safer and more secure when they're inside. Mesh crates provide privacy for dogs and are the most portable, but they aren't very durable. Some dogs chew through them and escape.

Comfy Crate

After choosing which kind of crate to use, it's important to make the new crate comfortable. Put it in a room where you spend lots of time, but out of the way of foot traffic. Next, put a soft bed or blanket and a toy or two inside. You can even put a shirt you've recently worn into the crate so your dog will feel comforted by your scent. (If your dog likes to chew fabric, you can skip this part.) If you purchase a wire crate for your dog, she might like to have a blanket or towel draped over it to create a more "den - like" feel.

CRATE TRAINING A PUPPY

FRIDAY NIGHT: BEFORE YOU START TRAINING

The most important part of crate training is teaching your dog to associate her crate with things she loves. Try the ideas below to convince your dog that her new crate is the place to be:

The Treat Fairy

Leave the crate door wide open and make sure your dog has access to the room where you've set up the crate. Every so often, when she's not looking, sneakily toss a few treats around and into the crate so she can discover them on her own. Use something that your dog will love, like small pieces of chicken, cheese, hot dog or freeze - dried liver. You can also leave an exciting new toy, a delicious chew bone or a stuffed KONG ® toy inside the crate. Periodically leave special treats in your dog's crate throughout the evening—and continue to do so every day or so for the next few weeks. If your dog sometimes finds surprise goodies in her crate, she'll start to love it, and she'll probably go into it often just to see if the "Treat Fairy" has come.

Room Service

When it's dinnertime for your dog, place her bowl inside the crate and leave the door open. Try putting the bowl in the back of the crate so your dog has to stand inside the crate to eat. If she seems too uncomfortable to go into the crate at first, you can put the bowl just inside the door instead. That way, she only has to put her head in the crate. Over time, as your dog becomes more and more comfortable stepping inside, you can move the bowl all the way to the back of the crate and, eventually, close the crate door while she eats her meals.

Prepare Supplies for Saturday and Sunday

Over the next couple of days, you'll reward your dog often for going into her crate. It's a good idea to prepare some treats in advance. Cut some chicken, cheese, hot dogs, soft dog treats or freeze - dried liver into bite - sized pieces and set them aside for later use. You can also stuff two or three KONGs, which you'll give your dog when you start to increase the length of time she stays in her crate.

Saturday Morning: Let the Crate Fun Begin!

You're ready to get started. Gather the treats you prepared and take your dog to the crate.

Step One: Follow the Treat

You can do the following exercises sitting on the floor or in a chair right next to the crate.

1. Give a cue to ask your dog to go into the crate, such as "Go to bed." (Choose whatever cue you like, just be sure you always use the same one.)

2. Show your dog one of the treats and toss it in the crate. After she goes inside to eat it, praise her enthusiastically and feed her another treat while she's still inside.

3. Say "Okay" to let your dog know she can come out again. You don't need to reward her when she comes out of the crate. She needs to learn that all good things happen when she's inside the crate.

Repeat the steps above 10 times. Take a short break (just a few minutes), and then do another set of 10 repetitions. After your second set, end the training session.

Step Two: Earn the Treat

Later on in the morning, collect some treats and bring your dog to the crate for more training. Now that she's practiced following a treat into the crate, try asking her to go in before rewarding her with the treat.

1. To warm up, do a couple of repetitions just like you did before—

throwing the treat into the crate so that your dog follows it. Then you can change the rules a little.

2. Give your cue, "Go to bed," and point to the crate instead of throwing a treat into it. (When you point, it might help to move your arm like you did when tossing a treat into the crate. The familiar motion can remind your dog what she's supposed to do.)

3. When your dog goes in, praise her and immediately give her a ouple of treats while she's still in the crate.

4. Say "Okay" and let your dog come out of the crate.

Do 10 repetitions and then take a short break. Repeat the exercise another 10 times—or until your dog seems to know the game and enters and exits readily when you ask her to. If your dog seems nervous about going into the crate or confused about what she's supposed to do when you say the cue, go back and practice Step One for a while longer. When your dog confidently rushes into the crate to get her treat, you can try Step Two again.

Saturday Afternoon: Close the Crate Door

Now it's time to get your dog used to being in the crate with the door closed.

1. To warm up, do a couple of repetitions just like you did before. Say "Go to bed," point to the crate, reward your dog with a treat when she goes in and then say "Okay" to let her know she can come out.

2. Now you'll try closing the crate door for just a moment. Give your cue "Go to bed" and point to the crate.

3. When your dog goes in the crate, praise her and immediately give her a treat. Then gently close the crate door. (You don't have to latch it yet.) Feed your dog two or three treats through the closed crate door and continue to praise her while she's in the crate.

4. Say "Okay" and open the crate door to let your dog come out. (If your dog seems stressed or panicked with the door briefly closed, break down this exercise into two phases: in the first phase, just close the door halfway, give a treat and release your dog; in the second phase, close the door all the way.)

Do 10 repetitions and then take a break for a minute or two. Then repeat the exercise 10 more times, slowly building up the time your dog stays in the crate with the door closed. As you increase the time, throw in some easy repetitions, too. Start with 1 second, then increase to 5. Try 8 seconds, then go back to 3. Increase to 10 seconds, then 15, then 20, then an easy 5. Continue to generously reward your dog whenever she's in the crate. After you finish your second set of 10 repetitions, take a half - hour break. Then repeat the exercise again. Over the afternoon, try to build up to having your dog stay in the crate for one minute.

Saturday Evening: Introduction to Alone Time

When your dog is used to hanging out in her crate with the door closed while you sit nearby, you can move on to the next step: leaving her alone for a little while. Repeat the exercise you've been practicing, just as it's described above— but this time, latch the crate door and start to move away from the crate.

1. To warm up, do a couple of repetitions like you did in the afternoon. Sit on the floor or in a chair next to your dog's crate. Say "Go to bed" and point to the crate. When your dog goes in, close the crate door and reward her with a few treats while she stays in the crate. After about 30 seconds, say "Okay" and open the crate door to let your dog out.

2. Now you'll close the crate door briefly. Say your cue, "Go to bed," and point to the crate. When your dog goes in, close and latch the crate door, and then give her a treat.

3. Stand up and give your dog another treat. Take a few steps away from the crate and then return to give your dog a treat.

4. Say "Okay" and open the crate door to let your dog come out.

Repeat the steps above 10 times, each time walking away in a different direction. After a short break, do 10 more repetitions, slowly building up the time your dog stays in the crate while you walk around the room. As you increase the time, throw in some easy repetitions. Start with 10 seconds, then increase to 15. Try 20 seconds, then go back to 10. Increase to 30 seconds, drop to 15, then up to 45, and then an easy 5. Continue to return to the crate and reward your dog every few seconds while she's inside. In the begin-ning, be very generous. As your dog becomes more and more comfortable resting in her crate, you can gradually decrease how frequently you treat her.

After you finish your second set of 10 repetitions, take a half-hour break. Then repeat the exercise another 10 times. Start leaving the room for a few seconds at a time, always returning to reward your dog while she's in the crate. Try to work up to having your dog stay in the crate for one minute while you walk around the room and briefly leave the room.

Sunday Morning: TV Time

This morning, you'll teach your dog to relax for longer periods in her crate. You'll need some treats, a new tasty chew bone or a KONG toy stuffed with something wonderful, like a little peanut butter or cream cheese, and something to occupy ourself. Ask your dog to go in her crate. When she does, praise her and give her the chew bone or stuffed KONG. Then close the crate door and settle down to watch TV or read a book in the same room. Keep your dog in her crate for about half an hour. (If she finishes her chew, you can periodically give her a treat or two, as long as she stays *q*uiet.)

When the half hour is up, calmly open the crate and say "Okay," so that your dog can come out. Take her chew thing away, and don't reward her with treats when crate time is over. In fact, it's best if you just ignore your dog for a few minutes. Again, you want her to learn that great things happen while she's in the crate, not when she comes out. Take a break from training for a while. An hour or two later, you can repeat the exercise.

Canine Complaining

At this point in your training, your dog might start to object to confinement in her crate. If she barks or whines, you have two options:

1. Ignore her entirely. (Get yourself a pair of earplugs if you need to.) She's trying to get your attention, so don't reward her barking by giving it to her! Pretend she's invisible. As soon as she stops vocalizing for a few seconds, you can give her a treat. With repetition, your dog will learn that she gets ignored if she makes noise, but if she's quiet, you deliver tasty treats.

2. As soon as your dog starts to bark or whine, make some sort of noise to let her know that she's made a mistake. You can say "Oops!" or "Too bad," and then immediately leave the room. Don't come back until your dog has been quiet for at least 5 to 10 seconds. With repetition, your dog will learn that making noise makes you instantly leave but being quiet makes you come back.

It's important that you respond consistently when your dog makes noise in her crate. It might be frustrating at first, but if you stick to your plan, she'll learn that it's in her best interest to rest quietly when crated.

Sunday Afternoon: Alone Time

Before moving on to Sunday afternoon exercises, give your dog a good workout. Take her outside on a brisk walk or jog, play fetch or tug, or give her a chance to play with a dog buddy. Crate training will be easier if she's tired. After you've exercised your dog, repeat the training steps you practiced this morning, but this time, instead of settling down to relax in the same room as your dog, you'll move around the house.

1. Ask your dog to go in her crate. When she does, hand her a delicious chew bone or a stuffed KONG. Then close the crate door and walk out of the room.

2. Stay out of the room for 10 minutes. After the time's up, you can return and let your dog out of the crate. (If she hasn't finished working on her chew thing, take it away after she leaves the crate. She only gets special goodies during crate time.) If your dog makes noise in the crate while you're gone, don't return to let her out until she's been quiet for 5 to 10 seconds.

3. After a short break, repeat the exercise.

This afternoon, continue to repeat the steps above, slowly building up the time your dog stays in her crate. Try to work up to one full hour of alone time.

Sunday Evening: Time to Leave the House

If your dog can quietly rest in her crate for an hour while you move around the house, you're ready to leave her home alone. Ask your dog to go in her crate and give her something delicious to chew or eat, just like you did before. Then close the crate and, without saying any goodbyes, leave the house for about 10 minutes. When you return, calmly let your dog out of her crate and take away her chew. Resist the urge to celebrate. Your dog will feel most comfortable going into and out of her crate if you act like it's no big deal.

Repeat the exercise as often as possible before bedtime, with exercise and potty breaks in between training times. Try to build up to leaving your dog in her crate, home alone, for an hour or two.

The Weekend's Over... What Next?

Now that you've completed the Weekend Crate Training plan, your dog can start to stay in her crate whenever you leave the house, overnight and when you can't directly supervise her during the day. Abide by the crate duration guidelines above, and keep the following tips in mind to make sure your dog continues to feel comfortable in the crate:

• Always try to thoroughly exercise your dog before crating her. (Aim for at least 30 to 60 minutes of aerobic exercise.) If you crate your dog while you're at work and overnight, she'll need lots of quality play time and exercise with you when she's not in her crate. Always take your dog out for a potty break before crating her and right after letting her out of the crate.

• Continue to feed your dog her meals inside the crate and always leave her with something to chew when she's in her crate. (Speak with your veterinarian for advice about what's safe for your dog to chew while she's alone.) If you reserve special things, like dinner, new chew bones, stuffed KONGs and pig ears for crate time, your dog will learn to love going into her crate.

• Leave your dog's crate open so that she can access it at all times. Many dogs choose to rest inside their crates even when they don't have to.

Having Trouble?

Crate training can be challenging for some dogs. A professional trainer will offer group or private classes that can provide lots of help with crate training.

POSSIBLE PROBL

WHINING

*I*f your dog whines or cries at night while he is in his crate, it is difficult to separate the reasons for his actions.

Questions you need to ask yourself:

1. Did he go potty before bedtime?
2. Was he fed?
3. Is he comfortable - cold or hot?

This process of elimination determines the first step of troubleshooting the whining and crying. If it is none of the above, try ignoring him. If you have not rewarded him in the past for his behavior by letting him out of his dog crate, then I cannot emphasize enough - Do Not Start. If he continues whining, after about 10 minutes, ask him your command word for potty. If he gets excited, take him outside, but make sure it is business only and not playtime. Make it short and return him to his crate without scolding or fuss. If you are convinced he doesn't need to go potty, ignore the whining until it stops. Don't give in. He learns very quickly that he can break you down no matter how long he has to whine to get out. Trust me; they can go on forever if they think they have the slightest chance. If you have progressed slowly in your crate training, you should not is problem. If you end up with this problem and it becomes anageable, start the crate training process over.

Separation Anxiety

A dog crate will not remedy separation anxiety. Destructive abehavior, while you are away, is not something a dog crate will solve. The possibility of your dog hurting himself while being crated if he has this behavior is very high. Separation anxiety is a complex problem best left to professional animal behaviorists.

Spending Too Much Time in the Crate

A crate will not solve problems. It can be a time out place if handled correctly with no scolding involved, but it is not a prison where a dog may feel trapped and helpless. If you work during the day and crate your dog, come home and let him out, then go to bed and crate him all night again, that is too much time spent in his crate. Arrangements to have someone let him out and walk him or a doggie day care during the day would help meet his physical and emotional needs. Puppies can be in their crate during the day for 30 minutes for every month of age. A 5-month-old dog should only be in his crate for a maximum of 2 1/2 hours at one time during the day.

If you crate train your dog properly, he will think it is his safe place and always be happy to spend some time in it when needed. This article is a guideline for you. What works for some may not work for you and your dog. Educate yourself and study your dog's behavior for a win, win relationship.

If your dog continues to whine, bark or howl in the crate:

Make sure you have introduced the dog properly to the crate. So many people fail to do this. It pays to start over, following the crate training tips in this eBook.There are various approaches for responding to a dog who protests being crated:

* The most recommended, effective approach is to ignore the vocal protests.

* The exception: if there is a chance your pup or dog has to relieve him. In that case, take him right outside, give him the chance to eliminate, praise for eliminating, and gently but firmly instruct him to reenter the crate. Make sure you limit the outing to strictly letting the

dog do his business; don't let the pup persuade you to turn the outing into playtime.

Here is one way to see if a dog really has to eliminate. First, teach your dog a phrase or command that connotes with going to the bathroom, such as "potty". Then, for those times your dog expresses anxiety or restlessness in the crate that might be signs of needing to relieve him, say the phrase ("potty?") and observe carefully. If his response indicates that, yes, he might have to relieve himself, take him right outdoors and limit the outing to just pottying.

* If the whining continues after you've ignored him for several minutes, use the phrase he associates with going outside to eliminate. If he responds and becomes excited, take him outside. This should be a trip with a purpose, not play time.

* Ignoring usually works, though not always immediately, since any type of acknowledgment of the dog -- talking, eye contact, touch -- is usually construed by the dog as attention. Usually, if the behavior is just ignored, instead of reward, it will stop...since dogs, like people, have a natural instinct to "do what works".

* The protest behavior may get worse before it gets better. But it will usually taper off and stop altogether. That is simple behavior modification, notes expert trainers. If a behavior is not rewarded, it will not continue. There will be no reason for the dog to engage in the behavior if he gets nothing out of it.

* Another approach: you can employ clicker training techniques. When the dog is quiet, click and treat. When the dog is noisy, leave the room and shut the door. This is a positive reinforcement approach.

* Some folks have success using a squirt bottle, though many canine behavior experts recommend using such aversive approaches. When the dog is noisy in the crate, quietly squirt the dog without looking or saying anything. Then quietly shut the door and walk away. If using an aversive technique, you would respond the same way, such as by squirting, every time the dog made noise, since consistency is key to training.

* Another aversive approach: giving a correction in a loud and/or

firm voice. Or knocking on the side of the crate in a manner that startles the pup, interrupting his barking. When using this approach, the goal is to have the dog associate his barking, whining behavior with the loud noise...so that he comes to realize that to avoid the loud noise, he should quiet down. Realize that a truly anxious or scared dog probably will not be able to make the association. Again, it is critical for you to properly, gradually and humanely introduce your dog to his crate, so that he learns that it is a place of security, not a place of anxiety and not a lonely, boring place devoid of environmental/mental stimulation.

* Stay calm yourself. Do not scold the dog; that only makes your dog more anxious.

* Realize that if you respond by giving your dog attention and/or releasing him, even briefly, from the crate while he is engaging in barking, whining or other undesirable protest behavior, that you are rewarding that behavior. Do not, however, let this keep you from taking a dog out of the crate if he needs to go to the bathroom. And you can also quietly, gently praise the dog when he settles down, even for a minute...since it helps to reward baby steps toward better behavior.

* Also, make sure the dog has had enough water. Realize that when nervous, a dog can quickly get dehydrated. Do not deprive your dog of the water he needs.

* After the pup quiets down, keep him in the crate for about ten minutes. Do not praise him immediately after release, or else you could unintentionally reinforce the idea that the crate is a bad place to be. After some 30 minutes have passed, repeat the exercise. Help your dog extend his calm time in the crate to 30 minutes. Gradually extend the duration of time you are absent periods so that you can eventually leave the dog alone in the crate for several hours.

CHAPTER 5. HOUSETRAINING USING CRATES

*T*he frustration that leads frazzled pet owners to abandon their dogs to shelters the most is a lack of effective house training. Remember that your dog is a family member, and as such, is worth the time and effort required to properly house break them, so that you can be a happier pet owner and your dog can be happy in their family's arms, not in a shelter.

Using crates as housetraining aids:

* Crate training takes advantage of the natural canine instinct not to mess where one sleeps.

* This technique is good for housetraining puppies as well as retraining many more mature dogs.

* However, in either case, crating is a temporary measure and not a substitute for teaching the dog and allowing the dog time to learn good behavior.

* And remember, pups can hold their urine only a couple of hours, and even mature dogs cannot be expected to hold their urine for hours on end. So it's unfair -- and cruel -- to leave a dog crated for too many hours. In addition, making a dog keeping a dog from relieving himself when necessary can lead to urinary infections and other health problems.

Housetraining hints in conjunction with crate-training:

You'll find more detailed, helpful guidance in the resources listed at the end of this tipsheet.

* Here's a snapshot description of the tethering approach: when you cannot supervise your new pup, keep her inside the crate. Whenever she is outside the crate, she is either being held by you or another responsible family member, or you put her leash on and keep the leash tethered to yourself or another responsible person. That way, you will always know when she is getting anxious; this typically is a sign that she has to eliminate.

* At the first sign of restlessness, take her outside to potty. That way, she will quickly learn that the place to potty is outside, not inside. If you can maintain this routine overnight, you will be able to housetrain your pup within just a few days!

In other words, a little upfront investment in super-close supervision will save you hours of housetraining time and drastically cut the number of accidents that any pup or dog has during the house/potty-training stage.

* Be sure to keep a schedule starting from the beginning of your relationship with a dog or puppy. Feed your puppy three times a day, gradually reducing to twice a day, at the same times each day. Instead of "free feeding," put the bowl down, encourage the pup to eat, and after 15 minutes or so, take up the bowl...even if the pup didn't finish the food. The pup will soon get the message to eat when her person offers the opportunity. More frequently, give her opportunities to drink. You can keep the water bowl down at all times, or provide it several times a day (don't forget...since pups and dogs need water just as humans do).

Particularly with puppies, you will need to take your dog outside within 15 minutes or so of eating and drinking.

Canines thrive on routine, so do your best to keep to the routine and your pup will naturally learn to trust and count on you.

* The first thing to do whenever you release your pup or dog from the crate is to take her outside to relieve herself.

* Stay outside with your pup in the yard, so that you will be able to

take the opportunity to praise her verbally and with petting when she eliminates. Try to encourage the use of the same potty spot at the beginning. These approaches will help the pup learn when and where to go...and that she can depend on you, her leader, to take her out before she feels the urge to urinate or defecate. If your dog does not eliminate right away, realize that this is not unusual. Linger outside, or go for a walk, for 20 minutes.

* Some canine experts recommend limiting water access in the evening before bedtime, particularly for pups during the housetraining phase. You can give your pup a little bit of water before bedtime. A smart tip: give some ice chips instead. This will occupy and satisfy the pup. Before bedtime, be sure to take the pup or dog back outside for up to 20 minutes so that she can relieve herself and get a bit of exercise, which will help her more easily settle down to sleep through the night.

* A reminder: puppies typically cannot hold their bladder through the night any more than human babies can. Be prepared to take your pup outside in the middle of the night for a few nights. This has many advantages over just letting the puppy piddle in his crate or on her bedding. Not only will you have fewer accidents to clean up, but more importantly, your pup will become housetrained much faster. Really.

* Avoid feeding snacks between meals and no table scraps. Use plain treats formulated for puppies. Do, however, reserve a number of little tidbit treats (plain, healthy bits of biscuits or pasta or kibble pieces) to use for supplementing verbal praise throughout the day whenever the pup engages in behavior that you want to reinforce.

Accidents in the crate:

Never scold or punish a dog of any age for having accidents in the crate, or elsewhere in the house. Calmly remove your dog from the room, then clean the crate with a cleaner formulated specifically for cleaning and removing odor from pet messes. Do not use ammonia, since ammonia smells similar to urine to pets, and your dog may feel compelled to mark over that smell.

If the dog starts having accidents in the crate, here are possible reasons:

* You might be confining your dog too long. Address the excessive confinement periods: enlist a trusted acquaintance or pet sitter to take your dog outside during your workday.

* You are not giving the dog sufficient opportunity to relieve him before crating him. See the guidance elsewhere in this tipsheet.

* The dog's diet does not provide adequate nutrition, or the diet is too fatty.

* The dog might have a bladder infection, a prostate condition, or parasites, requiring treatment from your vet.

* Past experiences might also be the problem. For example, some pet shop puppies become used to sitting and sleeping near their urine/fecal matter during their formative weeks. Puppy mill and pet shop pups typically are much harder to housebreak due to this reason. Female dogs formerly used for breeding in puppy mills are kept in tiny cages, and thus become used to being surrounded by waste. And some young, as well as older dogs, came from environments in which they were penned in or chained in restrictive spaces and thus forced to remain in contact with their own waste. These dogs can be retrained; what they need most are caring new owners.

* The dog might suffer from true separation anxiety. The separation-anxious dog can suffer digestive upset and lose bladder and bowel control.

* As in any aspect of teaching and training your dog, keep and demonstrate a positive attitude.

CHAPTER 6. CONCLUSION

*I*mportant principles:

- *A crate is a management and training aid, not a substitute for teaching your dog acceptable behavior. It is also no substitute for teaching family members and visitors how to interact properly and safely with a dog.
- A crate is not a jail cell, not if you are using this tool correctly and humanely. Confinement need not be unpleasant. Keep in mind that we confine our babies and young children for their safety and security.
- Humane and responsible confinement is helpful in the process of guiding the development of good behavior and habits and preventing the development of undesirable and risky behavior. That's why it's important to confine your new pup at times when you are not around to supervise him. Once undesirable habits form, they are hard to eliminate.
- The type and size of the crate should be geared to your individual dog. One crate does not fit all.
- The crate should be set up as a safe, comfortable sanctuary

in an area of the home in which the sights, sounds, and smells of family activity are present. A family room is appropriate. A dark and/or cold basement is not. Tight on space? Some folks place the crate, or kennel, beneath a kitchen, dining room or other table, creating a tidy sanctuary for the dog. And some folks have placed a tabletop on top of a crate to create more table space.

- If you're going to use a crate, introduce the dog to the crate on the first day the dog joins the household.
- Dogs like retreating to a cozy, secure den. In fact, puppies who are allowed to roam freely when alone tend to become anxious. That's why some get destructive; physical activities such as chewing shoes and scratching up floors and walls gives the pup an outlet for her tense, anxious feelings.
- By using a crate, you can support the development of positive behaviors.
- However, crating is not a cure for separation anxiety. It can be part of a behavior modification program, but crating is not a stand-alone solution. In fact, for some dogs suffering from severe separation anxiety, many canine experts do not recommend the use of the crate. If your dog suffers from true separation anxiety, gather information on this syndrome and be sure to consult a professional canine behaviorist. The longer you delay getting professional help, the worse the problem, and your dog's anxiety will become.
- Keep the crate clean. If your pup messes in the crate, change the bedding immediately. You don't want her to be so accustomed to sitting in or near urine, fecal or other matter that she thinks that's part of everyday life. That's no way to teach a dog to "hold it".
- Never use the crate for punishment. You want your pup or dog to have only positive associations with the crate. You do not want your dog to associate fear and anxiety with the crate. You can use the crate as a time-out spot, but keep the crate encounters positive.

- Do not overuse the crate:
- Do not commit the sin of over-use. Limit time in the crate to only 3 to 4 hours for puppies and 8 hours maximum for mature dogs. In fact, some canine experts advise that 6 hours is the longest that canines can reasonably endure in a crate each day. There is a limit to how long canines can control their bladders and bowels. And even though you should strive to make the crate a truly safe, comfortable, pleasant den, it still isolates the dog from the family and environmental stimuli. Without sufficient daily exposure to people and environmental stimuli, and without sufficient daily exercise, your dog will suffer mentally and physically, and this will have an adverse effect on temperament and behavior.
- You need to teach your dog how to behave properly in the house and interact properly with people and other companion animals in the home. Your goal is to gradually reduce the time the dog spends in the crate and increase the freedom of movement in the home. You do not have to give your dog total access, but the dog should be able to spend time in some parts of the home.
- The effects of excessive use of the crate include environmental deprivation, anxiety, hyper behavior (due to lack of exercise and limited movement) and socialization problems, since dogs truly need interaction with people and exposure to a variety of stimulation (people, places, other animals, experiences) to become a good, stable, well-mannered companion.
- Uses for crates:
- People use crates to:
- Aid in housetraining. Crating takes advantage of the canine instinct not to soil where one sleeps.
- Protect the pup or dog when strangers or multiple visitors come into the house.

- Provide a puppy-proofed, safe haven for young dogs when the people are out.
- Provide a secure, quiet environment for a dog recovering from an injury, medical treatment, surgery or any unusual or traumatic experience.
- Keep a newly adopted pup or dog from getting into trouble when you cannot supervise him. In a crate, the dog cannot chew on off-limits items or get ahold of something that can lead to injury or illness.
- Keeping your new pup or dog by your bed at night, close enough so that you know when she might have to be taken outside to relieve herself, but confined sufficiently so that she can't wander off to relieve herself in the house or get into trouble.
- Transport dogs safely in cars, planes and other vehicles.
- Create a home away from home when traveling and staying in hotels or with friends. Your hosts will probably feel more comfortable having your dog as a guest if you bring and use a crate, particularly for those times that you go out without your animal companion. In the crate, your dog will have considerably less opportunity to chew up your host's possessions...and wear out the welcome mat. (Be sure to push the crate far out of reach of bedspreads, chair cushions and anything else an anxious dog might try to pull into his crate.)
- Again, remember what a crate is not: it's not a pet sitter, it's not a long-term solution, and it's not a substitute for proper training and management of your dog.
- Crates can be used for mature dogs as well as puppies:
- Crates can be useful for housetraining and safeguard a mature dog who has newly joined the household.
- Even adult dogs can feel more secure in crates or a single room than with freedom to roam throughout a house. In the dog's view, it can be a relief to have a smaller domain to watch over in his person's absence.

REMEMBER

*I*t is both an amazing feeling and experience to have a well behaved energetic dog. However to achieve such a result you have to work and concentrate on your puppy so that when he grows, he is everything you expected. Crate training a puppy is one of the most difficult behavior training for a puppy owner. It takes a lot of patience and commitment to have a well trained puppy reading this book to the last full stop, you will be able to crate train your puppy like a professional trainer.

JACK REES

PUPPY SLEEP
Training

STEP-BY-STEP
PLAN
INCLUDED

Zzz

**THE COMPLETE STEP BY STEP GUIDE
FOR A HAPPY PUPPY OWNER!**

INTRODUCTION

* * *

Bringing home a new puppy can be a great experience for the whole family. You and your kids will be able to enjoy the new addition, teach them new tricks, play with them, and give them endless love. Many families dream about getting a new puppy for a long time before they take the plunge and they think that the whole situation is going to be perfect.

* * *

While bringing that puppy home is a great idea, many people start to regret it after a few nights of barely getting to sleep. Between hearing the puppy whine to having to get up and take them to the bathroom a ton of times, you are probably feeling exhausted and hopeless.

* * *

The good news is that this guidebook has the tips and strategies that you need to turn it all around. We are going to take some time to look at all the preparation that you need to do, as well as the three main strategies that work the best for most families to help them finally get their puppies to sleep. From the light sleeper method to the alarm clock method, and the heavy sleeper method, you are sure to find a sleep training strategy for your puppy that will work like a charm and will help you, your family, and the puppy finally get some much needed sleep at night time.

* * *

When you have brought up a new puppy and are ready to finally get some sleep and feel more refreshed and happy about having a puppy in your home, make sure to check out this guidebook to learn all the steps that you need to get started with sleep training your puppy today!

THE BENEFITS OF SLEEP TRAINING
YOUR PUPPY

* * *

*S*leep training your puppy is so important to everyone in the whole family. It helps to stop the whining from your puppy and can allow you, your family, and even the puppy to get on a good schedule together that also includes plenty of sleep. There are a ton of benefits to everyone in the family, including the puppy, for getting the puppy on a good sleep schedule. Some of these benefits of sleep training your puppy include:

- **Helps you to get more sleep**: If you have spent a few nights listening to the puppy and having to take them outside a million times each night, then you are probably feeling pretty exhausted at this point. While sleep training methods still take a few more days before you see them completed, they are the right steps that you need to take to finally get your nights back for some good sleeping.
- **Can avoid accidents at night**: If your puppy is up and moving and active in the middle of the night most nights, it is not going to be long before they have an accident. The more that the puppy is up, the more likely that they will have this accident. With a good sleep training procedure, you not only help teach your puppy how to sleep through the night, you also help to train them to go outside at certain times so you will deal with fewer accidents.
- **Let's the family sleep**: Not only do you need to get some sleep, but so does the rest of your family. If everyone is up in the middle of the night because the puppy is barking and making too much noise, it can be hard on everyone. Even if you are the only one getting up in the middle of the night to take care of the puppy, it does not mean that others are not hearing the puppy whine and bark and moving around. And it will not take long before this starts to wear on everyone nerves. Helping the puppy learn how to sleep train can really make a difference in the quality of sleep that everyone in the family is able to get.
- **Helps your puppy get their days and nights in order**: Just like it is important for you and others in your family to get enough sleep at night so that you are all energized and ready to tackle the day, so does your puppy. If they get things mixed up, they are going to miss out on a lot of fun

during the day playing with other people, going on walks, and more. Helping them learn to sleep through the night with sleep training can get them on a good schedule and makes life easier on them, as well as on you.

- **Allows the puppy to be comfortable in their new home**: When the puppy has some order and knows how things should be done and where they should do them, they are more likely to feel comfortable with that. And sleep training will make this process easier.
- **Allows for different times for play and for sleep**: You need to make sure that your puppy knows that there are times for sleeping, times for eating, times for playing, and so on. Some puppies sleep so much during the day that they get things confused and will have almost limitless energy in the middle of the night. Unless you want to be up with them all night and then head in to work, it is best to start working on a sleep training program with them right away. When the puppy learns to sleep properly at night, they are more likely to learn that day time is the best time to play.

WHEN IT COMES to sleep training, there are so many things to keep in mind. But remembering the benefits, and how much extra sleep you will be able to get when it is all done, will make the whole process worth it.

HAVING A GOOD DAY CAN SET YOU UP FOR A GOOD NIGHT

* * *

To make sure that you are able to get your puppy to fall asleep and sleep well during the night, there are certain steps that you can take during the day. If your puppy spends all day sleeping, and they do not get enough chances to go outside and go potty, or even if they eat or drink when it is close to their bedtime, then you are in for a long night. With some good planning and some positive actions during the first few days with your puppy, it will not take long before your puppy is falling asleep, and staying asleep, through the night.

* * *

So, the first thing that you need to do is make sure that the puppy is active and busy during the day. If they are an older puppy, or an adult dog that is transitioning into your home, make sure to take them on long walks, as long as they don't seem overwhelmed or stressed by the surroundings. With a new puppy on the other hand, you may not be able to take them out on walks yet because they are not properly trained to walk with a leash and they may not have their vaccinations to keep them healthy.

* * *

IF THIS IS the case with your puppy, then you will need to find ways to keep the puppy moving. You can play with the puppy, have some people over to meet the puppy, and give them lots of chew bones and toys to play with. If you are not at home and can't keep the puppy active during the day all the time, then see if there are some friends or neighbors who can do this for you. A dog walker or a pet sitter can be nice as well to make sure your puppy is as active as possible during the day.

* * *

NOW, some puppies are really energetic and love to bounce around and play all day. Others may be a little more mellow and may need some convincing to stay active rather than falling asleep during the day. Sometimes it is as simple as changing the environment that is around the puppy. If they like to get cozy in the house and sleep, then take them out back so that they can see the new sounds, smells, and sights.

* * *

OF COURSE, it is important to remember that your puppy does need a lot of sleep so some small naps are perfectly normal. As long as they are not napping all day and they get up and move around enough, then it is fine for them to have those naps. However, about three to four hours before you want to go to bed, do not let the puppy sleep. If you let the puppy sleep too much right before bedtime, they will have a hard time sleeping when you want them to.

ANOTHER THING that you should remember here is that what goes in needs to come out. If you are good about setting up a water and food schedule for the puppy during the day, it can help prevent surprises in the middle of the night. Most puppies are going to eat somewhere between three and four meals a day. You must make sure that this last meal is at least a few hours before they go to bed. This allows the puppy to have some time to empty themselves before it is time to go to bed. Three hours before bedtime is best, but try to not let it get any closer than an hour or two. If you are concerned about this eating schedule, it is best to talk with your vet to see what they recommend.

* * *

YOU WILL FIND that the whole process of feeding the puppy is going to need some trial and error. Not all puppies are going to respond to the same type of feeding schedule. If you find that your puppy needs to eat right before bed, or closer to bedtime than the three hours, try to make that meal smaller. This can help them to make it through the night.

* * *

IF YOU HAVE a puppy who wakes up in the middle of the night fussing because they are hungry, then pushing the eating time back to three hours before bedtime may not be the best. You can also try giving them some small snacks, like a dog biscuit, right before they fall asleep. This is a good way to settle their tummy and even a little water is known to help too. Just make sure that they are not eating or drinking a whole bowl right before bed, or you are going to be up during the night many times.

* * *

IN ADDITION, the area where you will put the puppy down to go to sleep needs to be calm and relaxing. It should not have all their toys around it and you should not spend the daytime hours making it fun to use. If you put in toys to the sleep area, you will find that the puppy wants to be playful and active. And if you play in the bedroom often, how is the puppy supposed to learn the difference between playtime and bedtime. There should be separate areas for play time and sleep time. It is fine to hang out or cuddle with the puppy in the sleep area during the day, but no games, such as tug of war or wrestling with toys in that area or you will have one confused puppy.

* * *

ONE PROJECT that you should concentrate on during those first few weeks with the puppy during the day is to teach them the command you want to use when it is time to go potty. This will be useful because it helps you to get the puppy outside and using the bathroom before bedtime. This will take a few weeks for the puppy to learn how to associate the word with the action, so be patient and keep trying. Then, once they have been trained with that word, make sure to use it before bedtime to help the puppy relieve themselves.

* * *

AND OF COURSE, you need to spend some time acclimating your puppy to their pen or crate if this is where you want the puppy to sleep at night. They need to be comfortable with the crate or the pen, otherwise they are going to get nervous and will not easily fall asleep. With a new puppy, all these experiences are new to them so take it slowly, follow the lead for your puppy, and show them what you expect out of them. But making sure that they have a comfortable place to fall asleep at night will make a big difference in whether they fall asleep and stay asleep, or if they are whining and causing you to be up most of the night instead.

* * *

IF YOU DO NOT HAVE a good day with the puppy, it is going to be really hard to get them to fall asleep for you when night time comes around. Think of it this way, if you spend all day sleeping, how likely is it that you will spend the night sleeping as well? Just because you were busy and active at work all day does not mean that your puppy got all that activity while they were home alone. It is your responsibility to make sure that they are worn out at night so they are more likely to sleep.

* * *

THERE ARE a lot of different ways that you are able to do this, and we did spend some time talking about them already. You are able to take them on a walk when you first get home. This is good for both of you to do. If you have a puppy, make sure to leash train them first so they are more comfortable on the walk and only go the distance that they are comfortable with. If this is pretty short, you could do a small walk when you first get home and then a longer one before bed to really wear them out. As they get older, you can make the walk longer and really get in some exercise.

* * *

PLAY TIME IS important as well. If you have children, include them in on this to have some fun. Have a variety of toys for the puppy to play with, both inside and outside, and just have some fun. You can play fetch, tug of war, or anything that gets the puppy up and moving. Just make sure that you simmer it down and relax a bit from the really rambunctious games right before bed or the puppy will be too hyper to calm down and go to sleep.

* * *

TRAINING the puppy can be a good idea during this time as well. This not only helps to get rid of some of the pent up energy that they have, but it can also help them to work out their minds, which can make them sleepy as well. Start out with some of the most simple commands, such as stay, sit, rollover, shake, and then build up or practice those as you are ready. Include everyone in the family so that they can teach the puppy some new tricks and the puppy learns that everyone can be in charge in the home.

* * *

OF COURSE, always remember to not feed the puppy too much and too close to bed. You do not want the puppy to be hungry, but if they load up too much on food and snacks right before bed, it is only going to be a few hours before they are ready to get up and be let outside again. Allow enough time before bed for the puppy to eat and then for them to go to the bathroom a few hours later to relieve themselves so they will sleep better.

* * *

AND FINALLY, take some time to make their room or sleeping area as comfortable as possible. With a puppy you just brought home, you may want to let them sleep with you and then move them to another area or to their crate later on. You can make that decision, just make sure that the puppy is going to be comfortable in their sleeping arrangements before it is time to go to bed.

* * *

THIS MAY SEEM like a lot of work in the beginning, but it is necessary to ensure that your puppy feels good and will get some good sleep at night. The more active you can keep them, the more comfortable their bed, and the less they need to go to the bathroom before bed, the better you will be able to sleep that night.

WHERE SHOULD I PUT MY PUPPY TO SLEEP?

The next question to consider is where you would like to put the puppy to sleep. This location is going to depend on you and your family. Some families like to have the puppy right next to them so they can spend more time together. Others are not that fond of the idea of having a shedding or snoring beast in their bedrooms, so they will pick another location. There are many options that you are able to choose from when it comes to the sleeping location for your puppy, and you need to pick the one that you think works the best.

* * *

FIRST, you must decide where the puppy needs to sleep, right from the start. This may or may not be the same area you want to use when you pick a spot for them permanently because sometimes it is best to keep the puppy near you when they first come home. Most dogs are considered pack animals and they feel more comfortable when they are able to be near other people.

* * *

THIS IS true whether you are dealing with a puppy or a grown dog. Some people choose to keep the puppy in the same room as them well into adulthood just because it feels more comfortable to the dog and can make sleeping at night easier on everyone in the home.

* * *

YOU CAN ALWAYS MOVE the puppy to another place in the home once they are older and a bit more comfortable. Even if you do not plan to make this a permanent thing, having the puppy spend the first few nights with them can help them feel more secure and comfortable in this new environment and can actually help them make it through the night faster.

* * *

IF YOU DO DECIDE to have the puppy sleep in one place and then you want to change that location later when the puppy gets older, that is fine. But you must remember that this is going to add in some more steps to the process. You may find that you have to retrain the puppy again to get them used to a new sleeping location.

* * *

SOME PUPPIES DO this well and it only takes a few nights or so to get them to switch over. Others may need to go through the process all over again to get comfortable with a new sleeping location. It is fine to go through this to get them in the right spot, it is just something that you need to keep in mind when choosing a place.

* * *

AFTER YOU HAVE HAD some time to train the puppy and show them how to sleep through the night, then you can make a personal decision about where they should sleep on a more permanent basis. You could choose to let the puppy continue sleeping with you as this is considered beneficial to them, but if another room in the home works better, this is fine as well. You can choose a place such as the laundry room, kitchen, or another chosen room. Some owners choose to let their dogs have free reign to sleep where they want at night, but you must make sure that you have broken them of destructive habits.

* * *

NO MATTER where you choose to have the puppy sleep, when they are young and first getting started, you must confine them in some way. Otherwise, you are going to find a mess, including chewed-up shoes, all over the home. Some of the places you can choose that will ensure that your puppy stays safe, comfy, and won't get into trouble include:

- **Inside their crate**: if you are already working to crate train your puppy, it is just fine if you choose to have them sleep in this crate. Just make sure that this place is comfortable for them. Add in a few soft toys for company, some good bedding, and that the puppy has had some exposure to this crate before you try to make them sleep in there. You can also consider turning the crate in a way so that the puppy is able to see you while they are sleeping.

- **In a pen**: A wire exercise pen can be a good place to put the puppy to sleep if you are using potty pads to teach them how to use the bathroom. You can pick out a pen for them to sleep in at night, as long as it is just large enough to fit the potty pads and the blanket for them to sleep on. This will help the puppy to figure out the sleeping and potty arrangements faster. If you use a pen, make sure to set it up in the area you want to use permanently to make the puppy more comfortable.
- **Dog bed**: If you would like to start having your puppy sleep in a dog bed, you do not want to just set it down and hope that it will all work out. You want to make sure that the bed is somewhat confined so that they are not able to wonder off and make a mess. One good idea is to set up the dog bed between the wall and your bed. This allows for a small area where you can place the bed, and then you just have a little space to block off with a gate or some kind of barrier.
- **In your bed**: Some people choose to have the puppy sleep in their bed, either temporarily as they get used to the new environment or permanently. You need to make sure that you are able to keep the puppy on the bed so they do not wander off while you are sleeping and cause a mess and so that they do not fall off the bed and get hurt. Most of the time it is best for you to just save this until the dog is older and can handle staying asleep on the bed.

* * *

AS YOU CAN SEE, there are a number of different options that you can use when it comes to training your puppy and where you would like them to sleep. Sometimes the method that you use in the beginning when you first bring the puppy home will be different than the options that you resort to later on when the puppy is trained and a little bigger. You can choose the method that seems to work the best for you and your family and for the puppy so that you can finally get some sleep at night.

PREPARING YOUR PUPPY FOR BED

* * *

*N*ow that you have spent some time learning about how to get your puppy prepared to go to bed at night and you have even thought of some places where you would like the puppy to sleep, it is time to prepare your puppy for bed for the best results.

* * *

As it gets close to bedtime, a little planning and preparation will make sure that you and your puppy will be able to get a good night's sleep. It is not going to work to just jump into bed and then hope that the puppy will fall asleep just like you. You do need to put in a little bit of work to see it become a reality.

* * *

First, there is something important that you need to consider before you get started with any of this. It is important for you to set a bedtime that is reasonable for your puppy. You must also have reasonable expectations for how long the puppy will be able to sleep at night. So, just because you put the puppy down for bed at eight does not mean that they are going to be completely asleep for the rest of the night. If they go to sleep at this time, then they will probably be up at two in the morning ready to play.

* * *

Many people have trouble with keeping their puppies asleep during the night and don't understand that perhaps they are letting the puppy go to bed too early. If you go to bed at eleven at night, but expect the puppy to go to sleep at eight and still sleep until you get up, that is too long. Most puppies are not going to make it past six or seven hours, maybe eight as they get older, before they need to go to the bathroom. It is usually best to schedule the puppy to go to bed when you go to sleep to make life easier.

* * *

While you are getting ready for bed, set out some of the things that you may need in the middle of the night. It is likely that when you have a new puppy, you will need to get up a few times to let them out. Rather than fumbling around in the dark when they are ready to go out, make sure that everything is set and that you have a nice clear path to walk through at night.

* * *

THERE ARE a number of things that you can prepare for this. For example, unless your back yard is covered completely and you live in an area that gets really nice temperatures, you should make sure that you have a robe or something else to wear while you are in the back-yard. You can also keep your shoes, your glasses, some treats, and other things right there in case you need it. If you are going some-where that does not have the best light, consider having a flashlight ready so that you are able to see what the puppy is doing and make sure that they will not get lost while going potty.

* * *

WHILE YOU ARE AT IT, make sure that the path that goes from your bed to wherever the puppy is located is as clear as possible. Tripping can be a hazard when you get up with the puppy in the middle of the night. You can even consider having a nightlight around to make it easier to see what is going on around you when you get up in the middle of the night.

* * *

ANOTHER THING that you can consider is having either a white noise machine or a loud fan that is ready to go wherever the puppy is going to be sleeping. This is a big help because the steady noise is really soothing for most puppies and is really good at masking some of the noise that are outside and may wake up the puppy. If you choose to use a fan for this though, make sure that it is pointed away from the puppy so they do not get cold.

* * *

YOU CAN ALSO CONSIDER USING a towel or a blanket. If you notice that the puppy seems a little fussy in their crate and they do not need to be let out to go potty, they may do better if you take the time to cover their crate. For some puppies, this is calming. Just make sure that you check the crate to see if there is enough air flow and that the temperatures do not get too hot inside the crate.

* * *

SOME PEOPLE HAVE ALSO TRIED another trick. For this, they will take a ricking close and a hot water bottle, wrap them in a towel, and put them in with the puppy to help make it easier to sleep at night. The point of doing this, according to some dog owners, is to help the puppy remember the heartbeat and warmth of their mommy so that they can get comfortable and go to sleep. The puppy will be reminded of their mother and the warmth and comfort that they felt when they were with her and for some puppies, this is the easiest way to get them to fall asleep.

* * *

STUDIES ARE STILL OUT on whether this one will work but if you like the idea, it certainly is not going to hurt anything to give it a try. You can even try using a plush puppy sleep toy that has a warmer or a heartbeat inside so that your puppy can enjoy a little bit of company while they are sleeping at night.

* * *

AND OF COURSE, the final thing that you must do before you put the puppy down, after their beds are as comfortable as possible, is take them out one more time to go to the potty. Do this about ten to fifteen minutes before bed, and then again right before bed, so that the puppy has plenty of time to go and can get all those distractions out of the way. This helps to empty out the puppy and can save you a lot of

ETHAN ADRIAN

hassle, and possible accidents, when you wake up in the morning. If you are dealing with a young puppy, it is likely that you will still need to get up a few times at night to take them out, but it won't be long before you can stop doing this as well.

* * *

SETTING things up so that the puppy is able to easily go to sleep can make such a difference for how much sleep you get. Make sure that the puppy does not nap too much, that they stay up long enough at night, and that they have an empty bladder and are as comfortable as possible. If you are able to maintain those steps and the other steps in this chapter, you will find that it is much easier to get your puppy to go to sleep, and stay asleep longer, at night.

COMING UP WITH A PLAN

* * *

*a*t this point, it is time to make your own plan for surviving the night with a new puppy. There are actually three methods that you are able to use, but before we get into a discussion about each one, here are a few basics that will apply to all the methods of overnight training, no matter which path you decide is the best for you.

* * *

First, you need to consider the situation and what your puppy is going through. It is likely that you got the puppy right from their mother and they are used to having that warmth, as well as the warmth of their littermates, around them. Even if you had a stray who you got from the pound or a shelter, you are still bringing them in to a new environment that they may be a bit cautious about.

* * *

What this means is that the first step that you should take for sleep training is going to include spending time soothing and comforting the new puppy so that they are able to relax before learning that night is when they should sleep. You most likely will need to let them sleep next to you for company, even if you want to have them sleep in their own room later on.

* * *

One worry here is that you will spoil the puppy and never be able to train them to sleep on their own. The truth is, the puppy will actually have a better time sleeping on their own later on if they got to spend the beginning time with you compared to those who were left alone right from the beginning. Even if you only spend a few nights sleeping with the puppy, it still gives them some comfort and confidence in their new environment.

* * *

Once you notice that the puppy is sleeping pretty good and you would like to get them to start sleeping on their own, it is important to do so in small steps. For example, if the puppy is sleeping in your bed and you want to get them to start sleeping in their crate in another room, the first step would be to get the puppy used to being in the crate during the day. Then you can move the crate to the side of the bed and have them stay there at night.

* * *

AFTER THE PUPPY has been able to do that, then you can move the puppy and the crate to their permanent sleeping room on a night when they are really tired. This is a day that you should really get them extra tired so that they do not nap during the day. This makes it more likely that the puppy will just go straight into the crate and fall asleep without any issues because they are too tired to fight.

* * *

WITH A SMALL PUPPY, you will need to get up and take them to the potty at least once or twice a night. When you do this, it is best to get them while they are still asleep or when they are reasonably calm if you can. This makes it much easier to get the puppy to fall asleep when they are done. If you wait too long and the puppy is screaming and freaking out, you will find that they are now too wound up to go to sleep and it could lead to a very long night for you.

* * *

FROM HERE, it is time to decide which method you would like to choose so that you can get your puppy to sleep well through the night. All puppies and their owners will be different, so you may find that you like one method better than the other, or you may need to do some trial and error. No one method is better than the other so go ahead and try them out and see what works the best for you!

THE BEST SLEEP TRAINING
TECHNIQUES FOR YOUR PUPPY

* * *

*A*s we mentioned before, there are actually three best methods that you can use to help get your puppy to fall asleep and stay asleep at night. None of the methods are better than any other, you just need to decide which one you like the best. The three methods that you can choose from include the following;

* * *

The Alarm Clock Method

* * *

THIS IS CONSIDERED one of the best methods to use because it is so simple and you will not have to remember a ton of steps to get it done. It is easy, but maybe not fun, but it is considered really effective and simple to follow with.

* * *

WHEN YOU USE THIS METHOD, you will be able to take control over the overnight schedule for your puppy by setting the alarm clock to help wake you up each night. It does not matter if the puppy wakes up or not. The point here is to beat the puppy to the goal. If your puppy wakes up before you, then it is because they are uncomfortable and they will probably get hyper and freak out, which will make it really hard for you to get them back to sleep in the end.

* * *

IF YOU SET an alarm and wake up before the puppy does to take them out, you are able to save a lot of hassle. First, the puppy will still be sleepy and easier to get to bed in the middle of the night when they are done. Second, the puppy never gets in the habit of crying and barking in order to wake you up.

* * *

WHEN YOU FIRST BRING THE puppy home, it is likely that you will need to have the alarm go off for you a few times each night. For a puppy who is between seven to nine weeks old, you will need to do this ever two hours. Once the puppy is between nine weeks to fourteen weeks, you can do it every three hours. And puppies that are over fourteen weeks will go about every four hours.

* * *

OF COURSE, these are pretty general guidelines for a brand-new puppy. Some need to go more often and some need to go less. Take the time to learn the schedule of your puppy so you can set the alarm at the right time and take them out before they wake up and get too hyper. If you have already had the puppy for a few weeks, then it is likely that you already know how long the puppy is able to hold it, so base the schedule you use on that.

* * *

SO, if the puppy has gotten into the habit of waking you up with barks and crying every four hours, then you should set the alarm for every three or three and a half hours. The exact time is not important, as long as you make it your goal to catch the puppy when they are likely to need to go, but before they get to a critical point of howling and barking.

* * *

ONCE THE PUPPY is on a good schedule of waking up at intervals throughout the night, you are going to work on pushing it to get the puppy to sleep longer. In the beginning, you may be tired for waking up so often, but this is the part of the program when the work will pay off. Since you are the one who is in control of the schedule at night, you are able to adjust the wake-up times and then work through until you get the puppy to start sleeping through the whole night.

* * *

FOR MOST PUPPIES, once you are able to wake up the puppy and get them to go potty at night on a schedule, without accidents, howling, or barking, for three nights, then it is time to move on. However, for puppies who are very young when you go with this process, it is better to wait for about five nights in a row before moving on.

* * *

WHEN YOU ARE ready to extend this, you will want to extend how long you wait before waking them up by about thirty minutes each time. So, if you were successful at waking the puppy up at 1:00, 3:00, and 5:00, you will now go through and wake them up at 1:30, 4, and 6:30. Once you have another three to five nights of this, you can increase it all by another thirty minutes again.

* * *

YOU WILL KEEP MOVING these potty trips ahead until the last trip that you have starts to coincide with the time that you want to get up in the morning. At this point, you should not be down to two potty trips instead of having to do three. And over time, you will go down to one until you are finally down to none.

* * *

ONE DOWNSIDE that you should know about this method is that you may get up more often at night and take the puppy to the bathroom more times than they really need. This is especially true if you start this from the moment you bring the puppy home and you have no idea what their schedule is about. In the long-term, there is nothing wrong with the puppy being let out more often than they need to go. On the short-term, you will miss out on more sleep, but this process does not last long and you will make it up.

* * *

The Light Sleeper Method

* * *

IF YOU DO NOT like the idea of setting your alarm clock to wake up all those times in the middle of the night, then it may be time to try a different method. Some people don't like the other method because they see that waking up by an alarm many times at night is stressful or that they are wasting their time by taking the puppy outside too often. The following method is going to work great if you are a pretty light sleeper and you are going to let the puppy sleep near you.

* * *

WHEN IT COMES to the light sleeper method, you are going to let the puppy tell you when they are ready to go potty so that you are able to take them to the right potty spots when needed. When you start to hear the puppy moving around in their pen or their crate at night, or if you hear a bit of light panting or whimpering, then you must get out of bed as soon as possible and take the puppy out.

* * *

TO SEE success with this method, you need to be a really light sleeper so that you can notice when the puppy starts to move around. If you sleep too deeply, then the puppy will start to wail and shriek to be taken out, and then they will be stressed and wide awake when they are done. In addition, this will teach the puppy that it is fine to wake you up with hysterics, and this will get old pretty fast when the puppy decides they want attention later on.

* * *

THE NICE PART about using this method is that if you use it the right way, you an save some hassle and will only take the puppy out when they really need to go. If you get one of those puppies who can go for longer periods for their age without needing to be let out, this method will allow you to get more sleep because you will not need to make unnecessary trips outside, resulting in a puppy that sleeps through the night very quickly.

* * *

HOWEVER, there are a few downsides to using this method. If the puppy does not move around a lot when they wake up, or if you find that you are not really as light of a sleeper as you though, you could end up with a puppy who will work themselves up to crying before you even notice something is wrong.

* * *

IF THIS HAPPENS, it is still a good idea to wake up and take the puppy out, but it may be time to rethink whether this is a good method if this happens more than once or twice. Another issue is that you may have a puppy who doesn't want to wake you or make a lot of noise, and who will instead just have an accident right where they are without you noticing. If this does happen to you, then this isn't the right method for your little puppy and it may be best to work with the alarm clock method to help get on a schedule.

* * *

The Heavy Sleeper Method

* * *

THE THIRD METHOD that you can choose is the heavy sleeper method. This is usually not seen as the most effective method to sleep train your puppy, but it can work for some people. This is sometimes the only method that will work if you have a puppy that is really fussy, loud, or resistant to other approaches. This is often a method that you will resort to when the others do not work.

* * *

FOR THIS METHOD, spend the first three to five nights sleeping with the puppy so that they can get used to being in your home and their new surroundings. When that is done, this method will require that the puppy will sleep in another room. Pick out a room that is at least far enough away from you that you will not be able to hear them crying. You can place the puppy into a pen, a crate, or a small puppy proofed room, such as a laundry room, depending on what housebreaking program you choose.

* * *

NO MATTER what room you choose to go with, it is important that you make sure that the puppy is getting a comfortable place to stick with. You should also make sure that the puppy is also getting enough chances to go to the potty during the night. However, if you hear the puppy scream bloody murder because they are not that fond of sleeping at night, you will just leave them in the other room so that they are able to cry it out.

* * *

THIS METHOD REQUIRES the puppy to be in another room so that you can ignore the crying and get some sleep. Allow them to go to the bathroom if they need it, but some puppies just like to be loud and fight going to sleep. This could easily keep you up at night and can make it difficult on everyone. If you are not a heavy sleeper, you can turn on a sound machine, a loud fan, a radio, or even wear some ear plugs. If you do this, set an alarm clock that is loud enough that you can hear it, and then use the alarm clock method so that the puppy can go out to the potty at the right times.

* * *

AFTER YOU TAKE the puppy out for their bathroom break based on the alarm clock method, put the puppy right back to the crate or pen or room, and then go back to bed. You will be surprised at how quickly the puppy will get over this screaming phase, especially when they realize that their noise is not really accomplishing it. Keep in mind that some puppies will get over this in a few days and others may take a few weeks.

* * *

THE GOOD NEWS that the puppy will get over this, even if it seems like it takes some time. It will just take each puppy a different amount of time. Once the puppy has resigned themselves to the fate and starts to sleep at night, you get the choice to have them stay sleeping int hat same area, or you can move them closer to you or to a new location if you choose. You just need to be able to get through the whining part and separating out the puppy from you can make that process a bit easier.

* * *

THERE ARE some downsides to this. The big downside to this is that if the puppy does end up waking up at night and makes noise because they really need to go potty, even if it is not on your schedule, it is likely that you are not going to be able to hear them. This means that you are going to run into a big risk of the puppy having an accident because they are not able to go out when they really need to go.

* * *

YOU COULD ALSO RUN into some issues with your neighbors that may not be happy with the wailing that the puppy has. You may be surprised at how far that noise is going to travel. If you are not careful with this, you could end up with a neighbor who is upset and banging on your door in the middle of the night. Before you go with this method, consider who else may be bothered by the crying puppy if you put them in another room and ignore them. If the puppy only whines for a few nights, you are probably fine. But if they are really resistant and cry for a few weeks, the neighbors are not likely to be that happy.

* * *

THESE THREE METHODS are meant to help you get your puppy to start sleeping through the night. Each of them will take some time to accomplish and will not get the puppy to start sleeping through the night in one night. But with some work and some dedication, and by following the suggestions in each of the steps, you will be able to get that puppy to sleep through the night in less time than you would imagine.

WHAT TO DO IF IT'S NOT WORKING?

* * *

*I*f you have turned straight to this page because you are already in the middle of the mess with a puppy who won't sleep, you may be in panic mode. You will not be able to go through and try any of the tips until you can read this book, and that will not happen until tomorrow. So, you may be wondering what steps you can take to help make things easier today.

* * *

THE FIRST STEP that you should take is to go pick up the puppy and give them a little bit of attention. Depending on how much time you have spent with them so far today and how active they have been, you may also need to go and get them a bit of exercise. Now, you may be thinking that this is a bad thing and you may be teaching the puppy that they will get their way if they make a lot of noise. However, at this point, you need to do it anyway.

* * *

FOR TONIGHT, until you are able to get some time to read the book and implement the steps that we talked about above, you are going to just give in so that you and the puppy can get a little bit of relief for the night. When you wake up in the morning, it is time to start it all fresh and use the tips that are in this guidebook. Since you have not even started on the training program at all, getting the puppy this once when they are crying is not really going to undermine anything. Plenty of people do this for weeks before they start on a training program so doing it once is not that big of a deal. Once you pick one of the above sleep training programs, do not do this anymore. But for tonight, so that the two of you can get some sleep, it is just fine to give the puppy some love and attention.

* * *

NOW, if your puppy did not get a lot of napping in during the day and they were pretty active, at this point they are probably tired but have just become too stressed out and scared about the new sleeping environment. You may find that the puppy will easily settle down once you let them spend some time near you. You can choose whether you would like to sleep on the floor next to the pen or crate to get them used to this new area. You can also tether them in the bed so they don't move and fall off. Sometimes moving the crate by the bed or elevating it on a chair so that the puppy can see you will help. Pick the method that works the best for you when it comes to puppy.

* * *

IF YOU DO this and you are a bit worried about how the puppy may wake up everyone in the family if you place them in your room, or you do not like the idea of letting a dog be in your room, you can just set up camp in the living room. For this, you would simply get comfortable on the floor or on the couch, and let the puppy sleep next to you. You can also let the puppy be in the crate and you can try sticking your fingers in to let the puppy know you are there.

* * *

THE POINT here is that many times the puppy will calm down when they know that someone is there and that they are not all alone in a new environment. You may have to be uncomfortable for a night or sleep somewhere new in the home, but it is often enough to get the puppy to fall asleep and then everyone in the home can get some peace.

* * *

ON THE OTHER HAND, if your puppy is still awake late at night and they did get plenty of naps in during the day, they may not want to settle down even after spending some time near you. This is most likely because the puppy has plenty of energy to use and they want to go and burn it off. The best thing to do, even if you are overly exhausted at this point, is to help them get that energy to go away. You can have some playtime or take them on a walk so that you do not have the puppy barking and waking up everyone.

* * *

No one wants to go on a walk or play with a puppy when it is time to go to bed, but this is the best option if you have a puppy who slept too much during the day and has a lot of leftover energy to get rid of. If you do not take the time to wear out the puppy, then they are just going to wake everyone else up and mess around all night. It may be three in the morning, but as soon as you get onto some of the steps that we talked about earlier, then you will no longer have to have this active time so early. Once you have been able to get the puppy back to sleep and settled down, then you can start to follow the instructions for puppy sleep training to get through the rest of the night.

Now, if your puppy went through a day that was busy and they did not have a lot of naps, and they are already sleeping right by you, but you still notice that they are freaking out, it may be time to change up the arrangements that you picked for sleeping. If the puppy is in a carte or a pen, they may not be comfortable in that yet and need to be tethered to a bed. Or, if you have already let them sleep by you for a few nights to help them adjust, you may want to consider trying the heavy sleeper training method so that they learn how to get used to their environment without disturbing your sleep.

One note, if the puppy is brand new to your home or they are showing signs that they are extremely stressed, then do not use the heavy sleeper method. If you notice shaking, trying to escape from a pen or crate in a manner that will hurt them, or lots of drooling, then you do not want to use that method. Instead, let the puppy stick next to you so that they do not get stressed out and then consider using a dog trainer in the next few days. You will find that severe anxiety issues like this are hard to solve all on your own without experience so if your puppy is showing these signs, it may be time to bring in the professionals.

* * *

IN ADDITION, if your puppy has been sleeping well and then they wake up all of a sudden with cries, this is considered normal. You should just need to take them out to go to the bathroom and put them right back to bed. You only need to go with the instructions that we talked about above if your puppy has already gone to the bathroom and is still freaking out, or if you just can't calm them down. You can always give them comfort for now and do whatever it takes to get some sleep, and then skip on to reading the tips in this book and following them later.

* * *

AND REMEMBER, while you are doing all of this, make sure that the puppy is not crying because they are hurt or sick. Sometimes the crying is because they are scared or trying to get your attention, and this is normal. But if you see signs that your puppy is not feeling good or is in pain and they seem to be crying because of this, then it is important to get them to a vet.

* * *

WHEN IT COMES to getting your puppy to sleep, you need to pick out one of the methods that we talked about above and then stick with it. Some puppies will learn within a few nights and others will take a little bit longer, but all of these methods will work. But if you just got this book and you have not had time to read anything except this chapter, it is fine to give the puppy some attention and company. You can always start on your chosen method tomorrow, but just try to get some good sleep for you and for the puppy for tonight.

* * *

The desperate measures

* * *

Now, if you have gone through all of the methods that are in this book and you are not getting good results after some reasonable time, you may be at a loss for what you should do next. It is rare for this to happen, but with some puppies it does. If this is the case, it may be time to take it to the next level.

* * *

AT THIS POINT, you may want to consider working with a professional dog trainer to help you out. Some will be willing to take the puppy home and do some of the initial steps that are needed for sleep training. This is only recommended if the trainer is going to have the puppy stay at their home, rather than in a boarding kennel. You should also check with the trainer to make sure that they have experience with doing this and that they have a training philosophy that matches up with your own. If you are interested in doing this, Talk to your vet or a friend to get some recommendations.

* * *

IF YOU ARE lucky enough to find someone who works for this, you could even have them do the first few nights of sleep training, or you can try a friend or family member to help. It is possible that you know someone who is able and willing to do the work and can make it a bit easier for you. Either way, it can take some of the pressure from you and make sleep training your puppy so much easier on the whole family.

* * *

Now, you may be worried about sending your puppy off for a few nights for training. This can be hard to send away the puppy and you may feel that you are giving up the responsibility that you should handle. However, in the real world, you sometimes need help and can't do it all on your own. Instead of having a few bad days and nights and then returning the puppy, getting some help at the beginning can make it easier and can make you and the puppy so much happier.

* * *

THE GOOD NEWS IS, that it is rare to find an adult dog that doesn't know how to sleep through the night. So, even if you have kind of a rocky start with the puppy and sleep training takes longer than you think it should, the good news is that your puppy will eventually learn how to sleep through the night!

AFTERWORD

* * *

Bringing home a new puppy is such a big deal in most families. It allows you and your family to bond with a new addition and can be a great role of responsibility for everyone involved. However, brining home that puppy can come with a few hard days and nights as you try to help the puppy get used to their new surroundings and get some sleep at night.

* * *

If you have a new puppy and you either want to start off right with some good sleep training techniques, or you are tired of being up most of the night dealing with the puppy, then this guidebook is the one for you. It took some time to discuss the different methods that you can use to sleep train your puppy and made it easier than ever to finally get your puppy to sleep through the night. There are three main strategies that you can use that will be golden and help you and your puppy to adjust to sleeping through the night.

When you are ready to help your puppy learn how to sleep properly through the night at any age, make sure to pick up this guidebook to help you get started.

CPSIA information can be obtained
at www.ICGtesting.com
Printed in the USA
BVHW031040240520
580228BV00001B/138